10D/new

(12)

(1)

KING ALFRED'S COLLEGE
WINCHESTER
———

To be returned on or before the day marked
below :—

-8 JUL 1977
27. FEB. 1978

14. FEB. 1983

-4 FEB 2008

- 5 MAY 2009

2 3 MAR 2010

24. MAY 1978

14. MAR. 1984

-6 MAR. 1979

28 APR. 1979

03. JUN

2 6 JAN 2012

21. APR 1980
-7. NOV. 1980

25 JUN 1982
MAY 17. 1983

2 4 MAY 2000

PLEASE ENTER ON ISSUE SLIP:

AUTHOR MOTLEY

TITLE Theatre props

ACCESSION No. 62)60

THEATRE PROPS

THEATRE PROPS

MOTLEY

Studio Vista

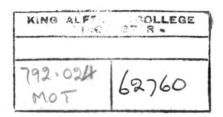
Studio Vista
An imprint of Cassell and Collier Macmillan Publishers Ltd.
35 Red Lion Square, London WC1R 4SG
and at Sydney, Auckland, Toronto,
Johannesburg
an affiliate of Macmillan Inc., New York

ISBN 0 289 70594 0

Filmset and printed by BAS Printers Limited, Wallop, Hampshire

Contents

Introduction

MARGARET HARRIS

> 'I will draw a bill of properties, such as our play wants.'
>
> Quince, *A Midsummer Night's Dream*

Why properties? The word, which seems to have been used in the theatre at least as early as the fifteenth century, is rather puzzling. In the *Oxford English Dictionary*, one of the entries under 'Property' reads: 'The condition of being owned by, or belonging to some person or persons. That which one owns.' Under 'Property, Theatrical' it gives: 'Any portable article of costume or furniture used in acting a play, an appurtenance or accessory.' The two definitions taken together suggest that properties are so called because they belong to whoever uses them on the stage. In fact, until comparatively recently, this was literally the case, as the actor supplied for himself such small things as he needed for his performance. So the word property, or prop, is a relic of those times, although now the professional actor is not expected to provide for himself, and the things that he uses belong to him only for the duration of the performance.

Currently, a prop is anything which appears on the stage which cannot be classified as scenery, costume, or electrical equipment. In the professional theatre, it is essential to clarify from the beginning who is responsible for each article, and a decision is usually made according to whether it can best be handled by stage, property, or costume staff, and which budget can best afford it.

Today the increasing number of open stages, and the attitude of dramatists and directors, is leading away from detailed, heavy, and naturalistic scenery. This gives more prominence to the props, which become an important indication for the audience of time, place, and style. With this lighter treatment the emphasis is firmly on the actor and his props, which all through the history of the theatre, have been more important to him than his surroundings, whether architectural as in the Greek or Elizabethan theatre, or scenic. If he can believe and have confidence in his props, they will become an extension of himself, and his performance.

> 'A man who cannot eat a property fowl is no actor.'
>
> *Pall Mall Gazette*, 1895

This is all very well, but the fowl must also be convincing. All props, in fact, must be well designed or chosen, well made and robust. No prop at all is preferable to one which is shoddy, inexpressive or badly made. Such props will detract from any performance, no matter how good. A good actress can mime rocking her baby in her

1 Making jewellery at the Royal Shakespeare Company in Stratford. Photo: Joe Bangay

arms, but if she is using a prop baby she cannot make the audience believe in her maternal feelings if they remain conscious of the fact that it is just a stiff doll. It must be the right size and weight, and have the same combination of firmness and flexibility as a real child; this is far more important than face and hands, which, in a prop, can never be anything but lifeless.

A door on stage may be of the utmost importance. The moment when it opens may change the whole course of the play, or introduce a new and vital character. The handle, which is a prop, must work and feel right; it must make the right sound as well as give the correct visual impression. This apparently trivial detail can help or hinder the truthfulness of the performance by the effect it has on the actor, and through him, the audience.

The best advice for anyone concerned with props is, use your imagination and initiative. Don't be content with doing what has been done before; invent new ways to get effects. It is seldom possible to spend very much money, and often things turn out better when there is very little, because this makes really hard thinking and a lot of improvisation necessary. Have a clear picture of what the prop should look like and observe intelligently how the details should really appear. It is often possible to adapt some inexpensive material or object to give a remarkable representation. Hard work and intelligence can usually substitute for money.

Responsibilities and approach of the designer

The designer is responsible for everything which makes the stage picture, that is to say, everything visible, of which the props form a large proportion, so it is for him to design them, or choose them, and to supervise any construction. Rehearsal period is usually short, so work on the props should start well before rehearsals begin. Whatever can be done should be done without procrastination, so that the furniture and props can be provided as early as possible for rehearsal. Once an actor has become used to a substitute prop, he may be very reluctant to change it. He may find, for instance, that he can work well in the substitute chair; the height and support of the seat suit him, and the size and weight are right, or the balance and grip of a temporary sword or walking stick may please him. Since these substitutes may be entirely out of style, and visually quite unacceptable, the actor should be constantly reminded that the real prop is still to come.

The director should be consulted about props and furniture at every stage, as, when the director and designer are in agreement, everything runs much more smoothly. No designer should be too proud to seek the help and collaboration of the director, who, after all, has the final responsibility.

Pre-rehearsal work

Lists

These are the basis of efficiency, and everything possible should be plotted and listed. A preliminary list can be made from careful and repeated reading of the script, combined with discussions with the director; but however thoroughly this is done, there will certainly be additions and deletions during rehearsals. A loose-leaf notebook is the most satisfactory vehicle for these lists; notes can be added or discarded at will, and there is no danger of losing individual sheets. A good practice is to select the most urgent items from the complete list, and to make separate lists of what should be achieved each day, even noting down the time each person or place should be visited, or each job finished. In this way, it may be possible to avoid being caught without enough time to finish what has to be done. But don't feel pressurized into making snap decisions. Wrong decisions hastily made can be costly and timewasting; it is better to give everything proper consideration, even if it means falling behind the self-imposed schedule. Do not rush, but never waste time, or postpone. The more that can be done without rushing, even over and above schedule, the more time is left for the inevitable emergency. Postponement or wasted time can never be made up.

Research

If a play is set in another time, another country, or an unfamiliar environment, it may involve long and arduous research. Though props need not be slavishly correct, in historical detail, it is only possible to get the right flavour by knowing the historical facts. It is always better to look for information in original sources, or reproductions of the original, rather than to take it from books where it is, inevitably, second-hand.

Anyone who intends to work in the visual side of the theatre would be well advised to build up a personal collection. Books on art and social history are, of course, of great importance, but you can build your own invaluable reference source by keeping and filing logically and clearly every available piece of information, especially pictorial, gleaned from newspapers, periodicals, catalogues, guides, and so on. Such publications as *Country Life* or *Americana* print useful photographs of houses and antiques, and most towns, historic houses and monuments produce illustrated catalogues, which can always be supplemented by taking your own photographs, or making sketches. And, of course, there are always postcards. Research may be broadly divided into three categories: 1. Period, 2 Nationality, 3 The unfamiliar and professional (subdivided into Realistic and Imaginative).

It is not always easy to know what to look for and where to look. General knowledge is, of course, a great help, but publications on history, social history, art history, and encyclopedias, will reveal the most significant men and women connected with a given time, place, profession, or occupation: biographies of architects, painters, writers, and public figures often yield valuable information in reproductions or photographs, and pointers to other sources may be found in the text.

Period

There are two yearly publications produced in Britain by A.B.C. Travel Guides Ltd. These are *Museums and Galleries of Great Britain and Ireland*, which gives a very full list with some information about the contents of each museum or gallery listed, and *Historic Houses, Castles and Gardens*, which also gives information about the date and contents of the buildings.

Besides the objects on display, most museums and galleries have more work put away. If you write to the curator, stating what you are looking for, he may arrange for an official or expert to help you, and, if necessary, allow you to look at the reserve collection. Allow plenty of time for arranging an appointment as it is never possible to hurry officials.

Nationality

Only the most fortunate are able to travel to the country concerned and study first hand, either in local museums, or in current use, the subjects of their research. This is, of course, ideal, as local atmosphere is absorbed in the process, but most people have to be content with doing their research at home. The first step is to extract what information you can from travel and topographical books, and books on the history of the country in question. Additional information can be sought from travel agents, who may have useful pictures of crafts, furniture, and manufactured goods. Most embassies have cultural attachés or librarians who will usually be very helpful; but time must be allowed to get the best from them, as they may have to send home for books and pictures. Foreign magazines and periodicals can be bought from good newsagents or the bookstalls at big railway stations, or they can be studied in the embassy libraries. Friends who travel abroad can be asked to send useful postcards and even to pick up books, pictures, and catalogues.

The unfamiliar and professional

It is worth stressing again the value of biographies, illustrated if possible. Trade and professional catalogues and other publications, if they are not available in the libraries, can be seen at the headquarters of the appropriate trade union or society; and, if their interest is aroused, members of the professions will be forthcoming with

9

inside information. It is remarkable how many people are fascinated by the theatre and will enjoy being asked to help. Nor is it too difficult, with a little tact and diplomacy, to see unfamiliar environments and places of work such as mental homes, coal mines, farm kitchens, laboratories, or the inside of a military plane or naval submarine. Some of these places may have restrictions about photography, or the light or camera angles may be impossible, but it is worth asking if there are any existing pictorial records which can be borrowed. Always go equipped with a tape measure or expanding steel rule, drawing pad and pencil, so that you can make drawings and record sizes.

For realistic plays the props should reproduce as accurately as possible the period, national or professional objects, allowing a little stage licence in the matter of size, clarification and simplification, but poetic or unrealistic plays demand a much freer, more imaginative approach. Some things required may have to be entirely invented. For instance, it is not possible to acquire much information about the machine in *The Rake's Progress* which turns stones into bread, or the banquet in *The Tempest* provided by the strange shapes.

All categories

Many painters, from the earliest times until today, have represented people with their furniture, appurtenances and ornaments, and there are many invaluable still-life paintings with wonderful detail, especially those of the sixteenth and seventeenth century Dutch painters. If it isn't possible to see the originals, good reproductions, plus a magnifying glass, will give almost as much information. There is a list of some of the most useful painters at the back of the book.

As well as being sources for art, history, and biographical books, most good public or reference libraries have periodicals which date back for many years; the English magazine *Punch*, for instance, is a very good source for the nineteenth and twentieth centuries, as is the American *Harper's Magazine*.

Some department stores have kept copies of their advertising catalogues from the time when they started trading, and an approach to the public relations officer will often lead to access to these valuable documents.

Old photograph albums are also valuable as they show everyday people of all classes and backgrounds and they often include details which are useful to the prop hunter. Individual photographs can be picked up quite cheaply but the albums are becoming rare and therefore expensive.

Having discovered how things should look, the next step is to decide on priorities. The props most urgently needed for rehearsal are, of course, those which affect the performance and the actors most intimately, that is to say, furniture such as chairs, tables, desks, and any props which may be awkward or difficult to handle.

The next decision is whether the prop is to be made, bought, hired or borrowed. A list of each category should be made, with the most problematic taking precedence. If anything proves difficult to buy or to hire, it should promptly be transferred to the making list, or it may get rushed out of existence. It is dangerous to be too optimistic, always hoping to find what you want the next day or the day after, dragging on until there are no days left.

Making props

The basic factors which must be considered before starting to construct props are size and weight, durability and fireproofing, the amount of detail to be included and the cost involved. Careful and clear scale drawings should be made, especially if the prop is to be made by someone other than the designer. It is advisable to make these drawings in any case; they can save time by eliminating trial and error, and the director can approve them before the actual construction begins.

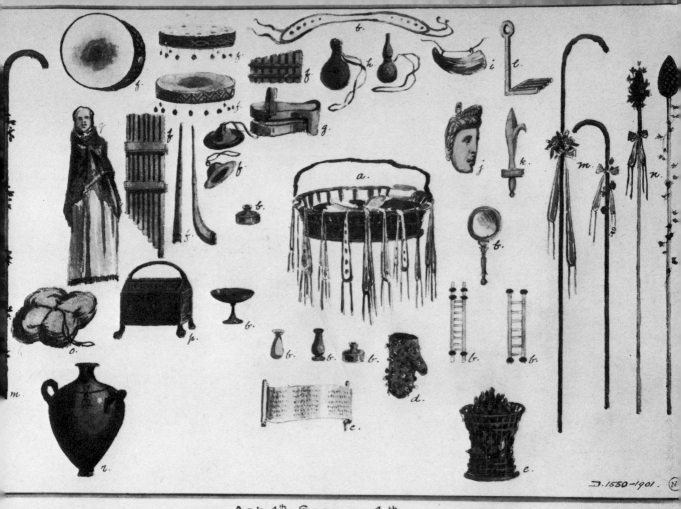

Act 4th Scene 4th.

Pedlars basket. *b. b. & c.* Trinkets. etc. in it.   *c.* Ballad.   *i.* Horn for drinking. *j.* Stone mask hung on tree.
Glove of flowers for do.   *k.* Sickle of Cronos or Time.
Basket of figs.   *l.* Key.   *m.* Shepherds' crooks.
Musical instruments.   *n.* Thyrsi.   *o.* Fardell or parcel.
For keeping time with foot. *h.* Gourds for drinking *p.* Casket. *q.* Infant.   *r.* Wine jar.

Size

The size of an object on the stage should, if it is something small like a locket, be slightly larger than life, to compensate for the distance from the audience and to make an impact. If it is a very big object, the size may have to be slightly reduced, as in the case of a cannon, so that it does not take up too much space in the wings or when it is on stage. The best way to ensure that the size will be right and what you expect is to look about you and find some object which is approximately the size you have in mind and measure that. For instance, the barrel of a cannon could be as long as your table, or a chair bigger or smaller than the one you are sitting in. Nothing, of course, must be made without considering the size of the entrances and the space off and on stage, or of the pocket or case, which has to contain it. Size relates very closely to its surroundings; if the scenery is very big or very small, the props must relate.

Weight

In principle props should be light; the staff can set light things much more quickly and quietly than heavy ones, and no actor likes to be weighed down by his props. But it is a mistake to make something almost weightless if it is representing something which would in life be heavy. It either looks absurd when it is picked up, or it needs a

2 Props used in Kean's production of *The Winters Tale*, 1856. Victoria & Albert Museum

11

lot of effort and good acting to make it seem heavy. Coal buckets, trunks, baskets of shopping, or dead birds and animals can be weighted with sand or shot, enough to make them hang convincingly, but not so much that they become a strain on the actors. The biggest problem comes with very large props such as litters, or big banners which have to be carried on. They can easily become top heavy or nearly impossible to manipulate or support for very long periods. The basic materials used in the main construction must be as light as possible conducive with strength. For example, aluminium (aluminum) is lighter than wood of equal strength, and bamboo is much lighter than either.

Durability

A prop which drops to pieces during performance is disastrous. However delicate and fragile it should look, it must be able to stand up to use; this may mean some faking or invisible, inside strengthening and some examples are described in the chapter on Special and Trick Props. Sturdiness, however, must not be allowed to become clumsiness. Use materials which have strength without bulk: nylon fishing line instead of cord, tubular members instead of dowels, thin sheets of metal instead of ply, hardwood instead of deal, and plastics in place of heavier fabrics.

Fireproofing

The strictness with which fire regulations and tests are applied varies according to the fire authorities and department concerned, but as public safety may depend on observation of the laws prop makers should know them and always comply with them.

The test generally applied is to hold a flame against the object in question for ten seconds; if the subject of the test stops burning immediately the flame is removed, it is considered safe. Some plastics may fail the test, not because they flame but because they give off poisonous fumes or smoke when they come into contact with fire; others are not allowed because they melt and drop scalding liquid.

Stage floors are dealt with by another of the fire authority's departments, and the rule is that the flame must not spread or run.

Some materials are inherently fireproof: these include pure wool, pure silk, hard woods and, of course, metal. Other materials are supplied already proofed for stage use: these include scene canvas, gauze, hessian, calico and duck. Plywood and 3×1 in. (7.5×2.5 cm.) timber can be vacuum impregnated with proofing but this must be ordered well in advance. Materials containing rubber, such as elastic, are impossible to proof as the rubber hardens with the proofing. The cheapest and simplest way of fireproofing paper, fabric, wood and any absorbent surfaces is with a solution of 8 oz. (200 g.) of borax and 8 oz. (200 g.) of boracic acid, supplied by any chemist (pharmacist), dissolved in one gallon (4 litres) of water. Brodie and Middleton, in the U.K., supply a ready-mixed fire proofing called Solution N.5, which can also be used on these materials. Both solutions can be brushed on or sprayed with a pump obtained from a gardening shop. For plastics, including foliage, you can use a substance called Albi-clear. This is a two-part solution, the finishing coat only being applied if necessary. Full instructions are on the containers. Albi-clear must not be inhaled and a mask with a charcoal filter must be worn when using it. These masks are obtainable from sculptors' suppliers. For live foliage a substance called Agricol is usually sufficient.

Detail

Props do not necessarily gain by being very detailed; too much decoration can be confusing, and simplification is often a great advantage. Sometimes an actor will find it helpful to have some small detail such as the correct initials on a dressing table set, or the real heraldic emblem on a ring, but such refinements cannot possibly be seen by the audience. Decoration should generally be rather broad and the design clear. It is obviously a waste of time and money to decorate the up stage side of a stage prop which never changes its position.

Cost

Every show has a budget and you should insist on knowing before you start work how much has been allocated to props. Given an overall sum it is possible to balance things out: a bargain will allow a little more for spending on some prop which is rather more expensive than expected. Anyone who works in the theatre is accustomed to the continual search for something 'less expensive'; whatever you find, there is always the hope that there might be something cheaper round the corner, but before you go round the corner try to reserve your find and make a record of where you found it.

The same attitude to expense applies to materials for making props. It is almost always quicker and easier to produce good props if money is no object, as the most suitable materials can be bought and this means less work. When props are being made by professional prop makers it is the labour which is expensive, so it may be more economical to buy the better material; but if the designer himself, or an amateur prop maker, is doing the work it is obviously less extravagant to buy cheaper materials and adapt them.

Buying and adapting

If there is enough money available it is sometimes less expensive in the long run to buy rather than hire. Such things as furniture, china, glass and cutlery, luggage, ornaments, and writing materials can often be picked up in junk shops, markets, or even Woolworths, and if the basic shape is right, or nearly right, they can be adapted by additions, painting, and decoration. If the props are to be provided early this is by far the best method, as every week of hire costs money. Besides this, a hired prop must not be treated or altered in any way, although some hire firms do allow a limited amount of painting to be done with water paint which will wash off.

Hiring (Renting)

There are several firms which carry an enormous stock of furniture and props for hire, and some specialize in props such as arms and armour, stuffed animals, or large plants, either natural or plastic. A list of these can be found in Sources of Supplies, at the back of the book. These hire firms charge a percentage of the value of the piece, so if it is valuable the charge per week can be quite high. There is also a delivery and collection charge and a charge for damage or loss. Hiring requires careful planning and should be arranged early, in case what is wanted is not available, and has to be transferred to the buying or making list. The designer should make an appointment and go to the firm armed with a complete list, and a clear idea of what he is looking for. He should allow plenty of time for this visit which may involve long and persistent searching. Once the things are chosen, they are labelled, and can stay in the store until they are needed. One advantage of hiring over buying is that things can be changed if they prove to be wrong; this of course means another visit and another delivery charge.

If possible the designer and director should go together to choose the most important pieces, or the designer can go and make a selection to be approved later by the director. If this isn't possible, the designer should take measurements and do some rough sketches, so that the director has a good idea of what is going to turn up.

Bearing in mind the difficulties which may arise through the use of substitute props, the designer should budget for at least a week's pre-dress rehearsal use of hired props.

Borrowing

Local people, both private individuals and shopkeepers, are often willing to lend furniture and props if they are assured that every care will be taken of them and that they will be promptly returned at the end of the run. It is sensible to take out insurance, especially if the things are valuable. Shops can be given a programme credit in return for their kindness.

Rehearsal period

The work of finding and making the props will, of course, not be finished by the time rehearsals start: it will certainly go on until the last minute. During rehearsals, the stage management make notes of everything wanted for each scene, which often adds to the already existing list. A wise designer tries not to let a day pass without dropping in to rehearsal to check whether anything new has cropped up, and if what has already been provided is working out satisfactorily. Watching rehearsals whenever possible is a very good safeguard against missing anything and it sometimes reveals exactly what would be the best prop to get for a special piece of business.

The director will be most anxious to see the furniture, because its size and shape will affect the ease with which the company can move about the space. He will also sometimes ask, for example, for a chair with a low or an open back, as this will have a bearing on the line of sight to anything happening up stage of it. An actress may ask for a very firm seat to a sofa or chair, to support her well and make it easier for her to sit or rise.

When the director asks for some special prop urgently, it probably means that an actor is having difficulties, and every effort should be made to get it as quickly as possible. It is important to remember that actors are under strain, they have to use great concentration, their timing must be accurate, and they are often nervous. Sometimes they seem clumsy and inept in handling props which the designer or property staff can handle without difficulty but it is not always easy to manage something when it has to be coordinated with the rhythm and interpretation of the text, and the exact timing and movement required by the director. The actors should be given every consideration, and their props must be provided in time for them to rehearse with them and get used to handling them.

The designer can enlist the help of the stage management in getting hold of props which do not require his special attention, such as newspapers, bottles of wine, or perishable foods. Such help often eases the time problem, which can be acute. Sometimes props are held back for fear that they may get dirty or damaged during rehearsal but this is very short-sighted. First, because it is very important for the company to

3 *A Man for All Seasons*, Globe Theatre, 1960. Photo: Angus McBean. All the stage props and dressing for all the scenes shown together.
From left to right: church door; ironwork gate for Hampton Court; leaves for a garden scene; rack for torture scene; hanging shelf with books, globe and papers for study scene; the Pope's crown; a permanent wooden screen

work with the props they are going to use in performance, and secondly, because brand new things look so unused that they have a very undesirable falsity. Things used in life are seldom quite pristine or straight from the shop, so why should they be on the stage—although, of course, it is always possible to antique them.

No prop should be used for the first time on opening night; there is too much risk that something might go wrong. For example, a snuff box may be slightly smaller than the rehearsal prop and go so deep into the pocket that it is difficult to get it out in time, or the lid may prove difficult to open, or will not stay closed.

Once the set is on the stage, the designer can start dressing it; setting the furniture in conjunction with the director, hanging drapes and pictures, arranging ornaments. This is the time for marking the exact position of every piece. However carefully the dressing has been planned, and even when every detail has been made to scale in the model, it is almost certain that there will be things to add or change. This is the time when the budget can fly to the winds unless very strictly watched: there isn't time to spend hours looking for inexpensive things, so the inclination is to buy the first good thing which turns up, even if it costs too much.

It is essential for the designer and prop maker to attend the dress rehearsals, and to make notes of anything missing, or which needs to be replaced, altered, strengthened, or mended. After the rehearsal this list needs organizing, notes made of what must be done, and what would be an improvement if it could be done. Good, calm, planning of the order and detail of last minute work will achieve far more than panic rushing.

Classification of props

Props fall into different categories and so become the responsibility of different people. Nothing on the stage is likely to find its right place by luck, and even the best of memories should not be relied on. Everything must be listed, plotted, and its position marked. It is the responsibility of the stage manager to make sure that this is done. In professional companies, it is usual to have a special assistant stage manager, whose duty it is to arrange and look after the props and get everything ready for the stage manager to check before and, if necessary, during the performance.

Stage props and furniture

These are often large pieces which have to be handled by the prop staff, and are usually on stage before the performance begins. They include furniture, carpets, curtains and their fittings, door and window furniture, carts, barrows, large trees and shrubs,

4 *Saturday, Sunday, Monday,* designed by Franco Zefferelli, presented by Stoll Productions and The National Theatre, 1973. Photo: Zoe Dominic. A well dressed realistic Italian kitchen set, for which most props were bought and then 'broken down'

15

statues, etc. The director and designer conduct the setting of these props in place, the director to suit the action, and the designer from the visual point of view. It is vital that the position selected should be marked on the stage before anything is moved, and it is well worth holding up proceedings until this is done, otherwise the whole process may have to be repeated. The most convenient way to mark is with coloured sellotape (plastic tape); a small piece can be stuck to the stage, and on it can be recorded what it marks. If it becomes necessary to move the prop, the tape can easily be taken up and the prop re-marked in its new position. It is only necessary to mark two corners of any square piece.

Hand props

These are things which are handled or carried by an actor and are generally smaller than stage props. They may be pre-set on the stage or they may be set off stage by the property staff for the actor to bring on himself. The on or off stage position of the props will have been carefully plotted, and the stage manager will check before the beginning of each scene to see that they are properly set. Once they are set no one must move or interfere with them until they come into play. If the actor brings a prop off with him, he must be instructed where to leave it, or it should be collected from him by the staff. Without this precaution, he may just put it down where it is likely to get mislaid. There should be tables for hand props off stage near the entrances, and it is a good idea to mark the place of each one with a label giving its description: 'Tea tray, scene 2', or 'Basket for market woman, scene 6'. Property staff, or stage management may have to be on hand to help an actor if he has a difficult prop to bring on or off, perhaps a heavy trunk carried on his back, or a very big banner.

Personal props

It is quite usual to hear the phrase 'Make it a personal prop', which means that it is the personal responsibility of the actor, who keeps it in his dressing room. Personal props are usually small things, such as walking sticks, or pens and pencils which are kept in a pocket, or note cases, money, note pads, etc., and although the actor is responsible for these, the stage management should also check to make sure that he has them before going on.

Costume props

These are worn by the actor and include jewellery, spectacles, watches, masks, swords, fans, orders, and medals. This category also includes parts of costumes, such as gloves, hats, cloaks, or overcoats, which the actor does not wear but which he may carry on stage either for himself, or to hand over to someone else. These are the responsibility of the wardrobe staff or the dressers, but again, the stage management must check.

Dressing

Ornamental props are not used by anyone; they are on the stage to give the scene character, or suggest period or place. They include pictures hung on walls, ornaments, books and papers on desks or tables, in fact, anything which dresses the set.

These are usually arranged by the designer, and must be carefully plotted by the stage management, who should either make a sketch plan or have a photograph taken of their arrangement. Sometimes it is more convenient and safer to glue or wire the props to the set or furniture. It can be very destructive of atmosphere or balance of design if the setting is not accurate, and the designer will be justifiably annoyed if anything is missing or wrongly set. Again, it is essential to have lists and plots as it is impossible to remember everything.

Light fittings

Light fittings which are practical, that is to say, which light up electrically, are the responsibility of the electrical staff, but any dressing of these fittings must be done by the property staff, who will also have to supply all non-practical light fittings. These may, of course, be either stage or hand props.

16

Hand Props and Soft Props

BETTY GOW

A hand prop is on the stage for the specific purpose of being handled by an actor. If the handling is incidental, if, for example, an actor takes up a rug and shakes it, it remains a stage prop, but if he crosses the stage carrying a rolled rug it is a hand prop. This is not quite so illogical as it may seem: the rug he shakes is part of the furnishing of the set, but the one he carries is provided for his particular use.

During rehearsals an actor becomes very attached to his hand props, and he should feel as much at home with them as he should in his costume, and they must, of course, be of the same style and period. His props should be provided early in rehearsal to allow him to accustom himself to them and to give the prop maker an opportunity of seeing them in use and time to make any necessary replacements, alterations or adaptations.

In an ideally planned theatre the prop maker should be provided with a large well-lit room equipped with running hot water, gas burners or electric hot plates, a big strong, steady table, a side table, shelves and cupboards for his supplies and a special heated drying area. In fact he probably has to work on the floor in a corner of the general workshop, or in a dressing room; he may even have to make the props at home.

However difficult the conditions may be, the working area should be kept as uncluttered as possible, otherwise more time will be spent in looking for lost tools than in making use of them, and props in the process of construction may get trodden under foot and broken. Many processes need drying time and somewhere must be found where work can be safely left to set. Always remember: not only is time money, it is invariably limited, so it is helpful to have all you expect to need ready to hand.

Once the method of construction has been decided upon, lay out sketches, reference books, tools, materials, paints and brushes at one end of the table or bench and keep the other end for working. Better still, if space allows, use a side table for the equipment. If you are working at night or over the weekend make sure that you have a good supply of everything you are likely to need so that work is not held up by shortages.

Basic tools

Good tools make work much easier and more efficient. They should be cared for properly and not used for jobs for which they are not intended. Do not, for instance, open paint tins with your chisel, or saw wood from which the nails have not been extracted. A prop maker who possesses the following tools can consider himself well-equipped.

1 Wire cutters.
2 Tin snips, for cutting light weight materials, thin plywood or chicken wire netting.
3 Pliers: round-nosed for shaping scrolls and arcs in wire (especially useful for jewellery work), flat-nosed for bending wire at sharp angles, or helping straighten out unwanted bends, long-nosed for lacing pieces of wire netting together by means of its own raw edges and for other intricate work.
4 Tack hammer and heavy weight hammer.
5 Various types and grades of files and rasps for wood and metal work (very fine files are useful for delicate work). A surform is useful for smoothing and shaping polystyrene or wood.
6 Various grades of glasspaper and a wire brush (invaluable for polystyrene).
7 Several different pairs of scissors. One sharp pair reserved exclusively for cutting fine dress fabrics.
8 Various saws for wood, including a carpenter's saw, a keyhole saw, a coping saw and a fretsaw. Hacksaws for metal.
9 Stanley knife or matt knife with a variety of blades. A scalpel or small very sharp knife. A really long-bladed sharp knife for working with polystyrene.
10 A set of wooden modelling tools. Apart from their use for clay or plasticine they are excellent for smoothing and burnishing foil.
11 Chisels of various bevels and widths.
12 A small spray gun with a replaceable pressure canister and a container for paint. They come with full instructions for use and are available from any good iron-monger or hardware store.
13 An electric soldering iron. This can also be used for shaping polystyrene which melts away from the heat.
14 A 3-ft. (1 m.) steel rule to be used as a cutting edge. An expanding steel rule.
15 Paint brushes of different sizes from 6 in. (15 cm.) to $\frac{1}{2}$ in. (1·25 cm.) as well as artists' brushes for detailed work.

NB It is never worth buying cheap brushes unless they are intended to be disposable. If good brushes are cared for properly they last a long time. They should be well cleaned after each use in a suitable solvent and finished off with warm water and soap. For short periods only they can be left up to their necks in water.

Basic 'consumable' items would include the following:

Adhesives
1 Scotch or pearl glue crystals. These provide one of the oldest and cheapest ways of making an adhesive and are still used where more modern methods would prove too expensive. They are stocked by most colour merchants. To prepare them, use a glue pot, which works on the principle of a double boiler. Add a little hot water to the crystals in the smaller pot and heat it over the water in the larger one. The steam gradually dissolves the crystals. Their potency depends on the proportion of water to crystals. The glue should be thin and creamy; if it seems too thick, add a little more hot water to it and keep it hot. There is an old rhyme apposite here: Too thick won't stick,   Too cold won't hold.
   If you are using this glue for polystyrene, cook it until it is partly dried out and very dark in colour and, if possible, use it in a dry atmosphere; otherwise it may take a very long time to dry out. When using it for sticking canvas to wood, put a thin hot coat on the wood and press down the canvas. Then dip a rag in water as hot as you can bear, wring it out and wipe it over the glued canvas. This draws the glue into the fibres and makes a strong bond, but it needs practice to become efficient at this.
2 A woodworking glue, such as Evostik w or Scotch Epoxy. (Should not be used for polystyrene.)
3 A contact glue, such as Evostik Impact 528, Bostik 1, Bostik 2, Uhu, or Weld-wood. (None of these should be used for polystyrene.)
4 Casein glues. These are excellent for wood joints as they fill any gaps as well as

cementing the joint. They come in powder form and must be mixed with water.

6   Copydex. A rubber cement. It can be used for polystyrene, but it dries quickly and is best used as a contact glue, i.e., both surfaces are coated and put together when nearly dry. It is also useful for other light materials and for fabrics.

7   Polycell. A gelatinous type of vinyl wallpaper paste. Good for scrimming (the process of covering polystyrene, wire mesh or other materials with scrim or butter muslin to make a firm foundation for finishes).

8   Cow gum. A rubber cement. The best adhesive for mounting or work with paper. It should be applied to both surfaces and joined when nearly dry.

9   Spray glue. This comes in aerosol canisters, but it is now considered rather dangerous and should be used with a mask to prevent inhaling.

10   Araldite. A two-part epoxy resin. Used for china, glass, metal, etc., when the join has to be very strong, heatproof and waterproof.

11   Tretobond 37, Tuff-Bond 9. Rubber-based panel adhesives. Obtainable from builders' merchants or insulation contractors. Excellent for polystyrene.

12   Chloroform. Will fuse perspex. It is difficult to buy as its sale is restricted by law.

Paints, mediums and glazes

1   Size is a less concentrated form of Scotch glue. Use as a medium for scenic paints or as a priming in the proportion of 1 lb. (480 g.) to a gallon (4 litres) of hot water. To stiffen fabrics, e.g. felt, 2 or 3 lbs. to a gallon of hot water could be used.

2   Emulsion medium, obtainable from colour merchants, can be used as a medium for scenic paints as recommended on the container. For a glaze it can be made up approximately twice as strong, perhaps in the proportion of 4 to 1.
P.V.A. (poly vinyl acetate) is the base for many mediums and adhesives which remain flexible and which can also be used as glaze. Of a thick creamy consistency, they spread easily with a brush or spatula.

3   Unibond (P.V.A.). Mix with water in the proportion of 17 to 1 for paint and 8 to 1 for glaze.

4   Vinyl (P.V.A.). Diluted with a little water and brushed over the finished paintwork, it gives a sheen and sharpens the colour. This is alluded to later as glazing.

5   Tenaxatex (P.V.A.). Obtainable from National Adhesives.

6   Evostik resin w (P.V.A.). Can be diluted for medium or glaze.

7   Scenic powder colour. Can be mixed with size or any of the above mediums.

8   French Enamel Varnish (F.E.V.). Excellent for hand props, it comes in basic colours, which can be mixed for more subtlety. It is also possible to get more variety by mixing in some spirit dyes. The colours do not fade and dry very quickly, and as it is a transparent substance it never appears dead. The solvent is methylated spirits.

9   Button polish (lacquer). Spirit soluble.

10   White polish. Can be mixed with spirit soluble dyes to make F.E.V., but the colours are rather more subdued than the ready-made ones.

11   Polyurethane. A heat resistant varnish supplied in a two part mix of a good quality resin and a hardener.

12   Dyes. Either water or spirit soluble. When painting with dyes on fabric, prime with starch to help prevent bleeding, allowing each area to dry before letting the colours come into contact with each other.

Useful stock

1   Polystyrene. For carving and modelling. It disintegrates on contact with glues containing acid. Use Copydex, burnt Scotch glue or Tretobond 37.

2   Plaster of paris. For moulds and casts.

3   Alabastine. A filler.

4   Polyfilla. Used as a filler or to smooth over surfaces. Utensils must be kept absolutely clean and free from hardened residue as it speeds up hardening too much on a fresh mix.

5 Fibreglass resin. Can be bought already mixed with a catalyst; fibreglass matting; hardener. A hardener specially for use in damp conditions is also available. Directions for use are on the packet, obtainable from sculptors' suppliers.
6 Felt stiffener. Available from milliners' suppliers.
7 All types of wire. Galvanized, steel, brass, copper, fuse, hat wire and milliners' flat wire and flower wire (used by florists).

Fabrics
1 Felt. In various thicknesses and colours. Many uses for both the carpet and dress variety are described in the text.
2 Butter muslin. For scrimming.
3 Scrim. For coarser scrimming.
4 Hessian. For rough work.
5 Calico. Both white and unbleached for cushion covers, sheets and other bedding as well as many other uses.
6 Heavy thick felt or cotton waste wadding.
7 Dacron, plastic wadding.
8 Rolls of stockinet.

These are the fabrics most frequently needed. Others can be bought or may be obtained, in small quantities, from the wardrobe department.

Breaking down

A prop can look very good in the prop shop but the effect may not carry when it appears on stage. Under lights the detail may not be marked enough, embossed or curved surfaces may flatten, and the colour may be too bright or too light.

Just as an actor makes up his face to achieve the right visual impact, so certain props will need 'breaking down' to accentuate detail, giving them depth, or simply to make them look old and worn. Signs of wear and dirt must be applied carefully and thoughtfully. Observation and imagination will help you produce convincing effects of time and wear. It is obvious, for example, that it is not only colour which alters but shape as well: metal bends and dents, wood and upholstery sag, fabrics stretch, and so on. (The best way to get the effect of this distortion, incidentally, is to build it into the original construction.)

Metal
Added emphasis can be given to both real and faked metal by subtle painting and shadowing with F.E.V., using a fine sable brush. On embossed surfaces it is best to spray the entire area with the appropriate shadow colour (black for silver, brown for gold, etc.) from an aerosol canister or with F.E.V. from a spray gun. Then, with a rag moistened with methylated spirits, rub off all the top surfaces, leaving the inset areas dark. The foils and paints used to simulate various metals are usually far from the true metal colours. This can be corrected with a faint wash of F.E.V., of a suitable colour, well diluted with methylated spirits. It can be applied as a finishing touch to the highlight surfaces, or to create darker shadows on the under-surfaces and around rims and handles, giving relief to the design and shape.

Wood
On hired furniture and props the wood cannot, of course, be treated, except perhaps with a little water paint which can be washed off, but if the pieces have been bought or made there is plenty to be done. The sharpness of corners can be slightly rounded off with a surform or glasspaper or sandpaper. The polish can be sanded down, and the surfaces scratched, chipped or scuffed. Then, as with metal, the whole surface can be painted or sprayed with a dark colour, which should be rubbed off again before it is dry, leaving the recessed scratches, etc., dark. To give the effect of dust on furniture, a light grey paint should be sprayed on rather sparingly; powder or Fuller's earth can

be sprinkled on surfaces from which dust has to be removed during the action. For the treatment of 'weathered' wood, see chapter on Carpentry Props.

Fabrics

If necessary, these should be dyed a basic colour before making up, but it is better to add the breaking down after completion when the eye can judge where it will look most effective.

Upholstery, having been padded up to the right shapes, can be sprayed or brushed with darker tones of the original colour, especially under arm rests and on other areas which would not have faded. Faded effects can be applied to the piece using a pad soaked in household bleach. Old bedding of the bunk-house or palliasse type can be aged by using a top covering of hessian or burlap over a mattress cover of dyed calico. The hessian responds well to glasspapering and may be broken down in colour with F.E.V. or dye, both of which remain flexible. When preparing dyes, the addition of a tablespoonful of salt to half a gallon (2 litres) of solution should ensure that colours are 'fast'. Most dyes are sold with instructions for preparation.

Miscellaneous

China, glass and paper can be broken down reasonably effectively by spraying with a thin film of grey paint. Or they can be sprayed with glue and then sprinkled with powder, the surplus being shaken off when the glue has set. The edges of papers and holes in fabrics can be burned. Cobwebs can be produced in various ways. Butter muslin dyed a dusty grey, then sandpapered and shredded, can be draped over the props. Grey silk chiffon gives a better effect but is very expensive. Scara-web, stocked by gardening shops, also makes excellent cobwebs. Dacron wadding can be fluffed out and sprayed grey to make accumulations of dust. Greasy marks can be made with shoe polish, or by actually applying vaseline. Shoe polish is also good for creating shine caused by wear. Mirrors which would reflect light into the audience can be sprayed with black paint from an aerosol can. The old-fashioned method of soaping the mirror looks very artificial.

Practical props

These should always be designed and made in such a way that the actor can handle or operate them without difficulty. If a box, jewel-case, or piece of luggage has to be opened on stage, the fastenings and hinges must function easily, for obvious reasons. To avoid mishaps with locks and keys it is much safer to make a dummy lock. If a lid is required to stay open at a given angle, the hinges can be pinched with pliers, to compress them and make them rather stiff, or a chain or cord of the appropriate length can be fixed between the inner wall of one side of the box and a corresponding point on the lid. Alternatively, one could use the type of bracket used in modern briefcases, which prevents the lid from falling back.

Velcro can be used for dummy fastenings on bags, or other soft props, but it makes a very characteristic tearing sound when it is pulled apart, so the moment when this happens should be carefully timed. Knots in rope can be faked with a big press stud (snap fastener) sewn under the knot (in which case the actor must mask the action of 'untying') or a permanent loop can be made in one end of the rope and the other end passed through and tucked under, allowing no possibility of its becoming tightened.

Food which has actually to be eaten on the stage is also 'practical'. It should not fill the actor's mouth so that he finds it difficult to speak, nor should it be so dry that it might cause him to choke. Banana is quite easy to cope with: it can be mashed to look like cream or ice cream, or sliced longways to look like chicken or any other white meat. There are occasions when a real meal has to be eaten; this is prepared by the property master, and obviously the director must work round the consuming of the food. The usual substitute for wine on the stage is blackcurrant juice for red, or weak lime juice for white. Whisky is cold tea or burnt sugar; gin or vodka are, of course, plain water. Fizzy drinks can be ginger ale or lemonade.

A book shelf will often be dressed with dummy books, but if there is a point in the action when one of the books has to be taken out, a box must be made in the appropriate place in the dummy run and a real book slipped in. The book should be marked in some way so that the actor can identify it.

Prop vessels which have to contain liquid must either be made of rubber or a rubber bag can be dropped inside and fixed firmly round the spout or neck; if the liquid is not for drinking a fibreglass vessel will hold it successfully.

Metal props

It is rarely possible to make elaborate props of real metals. Simulated gold, silver, copper or iron may be called upon for a variety of props ranging from jewel boxes, picture frames, goblets, coffee pots and hand mirrors to statuettes, idols and knobs on swagger canes. These never look convincing if painted with conventional gold or silver paint, but if the budget is low, this method can be improved upon by the application of Dutch metal to prominent surfaces to suggest highlights. Paint dealers or artists' suppliers usually stock Dutch metal which comes in booklet form, with pages of gold or silver film stuck to paper tissue. To transfer the film to the prop, simply brush the surface with button polish, clear varnish or aerosol spray glue and leave it until it is tacky. Apply the metal film face down on the tacky surface, and rub the tissue backing with a stiff brush. Remove the tissue and use the brush to flick away any metal that has not adhered. An adhesive-backed metal foil gives a more realistic metallic effect. It may be applied in manageable strips to large flat surfaces such as tea trays but for small or intricate items it is better torn into small pieces and rubbed or burnished on smoothly with a wooden modelling tool. If an embossed or tooled finish is wanted, a bold-patterned lace may first be applied to the object with fibreglass resin, allowing it time to set before burnishing the metal foil over it. The resin is prepared as described in the chapter on Moulding and Casting, but in this case no matting is required. Copper foil can be used in the same way for copper objects and gold foil is equally effective for brass. Iron and brass are discussed in the article on Jewellery. Metal foil can be applied over wood, polystyrene, felt hardened with resin, fibreglass, in fact any material which is rigid and not too porous.

Documents

If paper props, documents, scrolls, etc., are used to dress a scene, then they must be fireproofed. If they are personal props, fireproofing is not necessary, nor is any special treatment needed for letters, bills and scripts used in a modern setting.

Modern paper, however, unless it is hand made and consequently very expensive will not be suitable in a period setting, and a convincing alternative must be found. Paper as a writing material was in use in the fifteenth century, but for important documents it was normal to use parchment, which was, of course, made from skins. A very authentic mottled parchment effect can be obtained by treating holland linen (the starched variety used for window blinds) with button polish dabbed on with a sponge. Since the edges of paper and parchment were not clean cut, they should be pinked with scissors. If they are to appear old, a dark brown F.E.V. diluted with meth can be sprayed on the edges with a mouth spray; for a tattered effect, the edges and corners can be burned. For very ancient scrolls and communications, a thin white felt saturated with button polish or diluted size will, when dry, look most convincing. The edges should be shaped while it is still wet.

To achieve the effect of a rolled scroll, cut three pieces of ribbon, one short, the other two fairly long. Stick them together near the top, with the short ribbon at the inside, as indicated in the diagram, and fix the seal to the outside ribbon at x. Stitch piece of Velcro to the inside of the short ribbon, and stick another piece to the scroll. Wrap the short ribbon round the scroll.

Period writing should be done with a calligrapher's pen, and these are available from artists' suppliers, with nibs ranging from very broad to very fine. Illuminate

5   Burnishing foil on to a spear

22

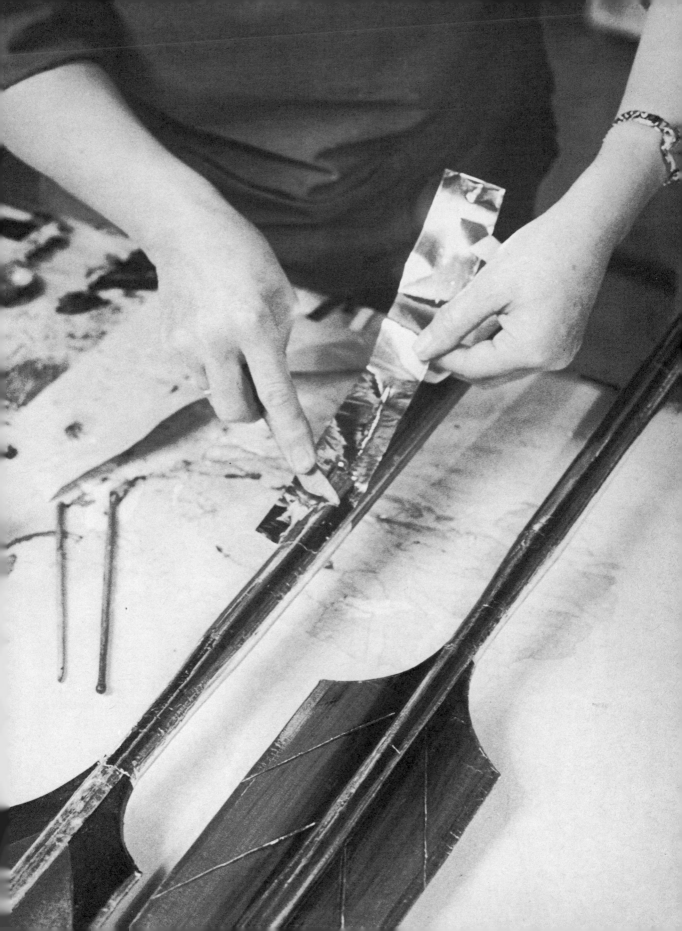

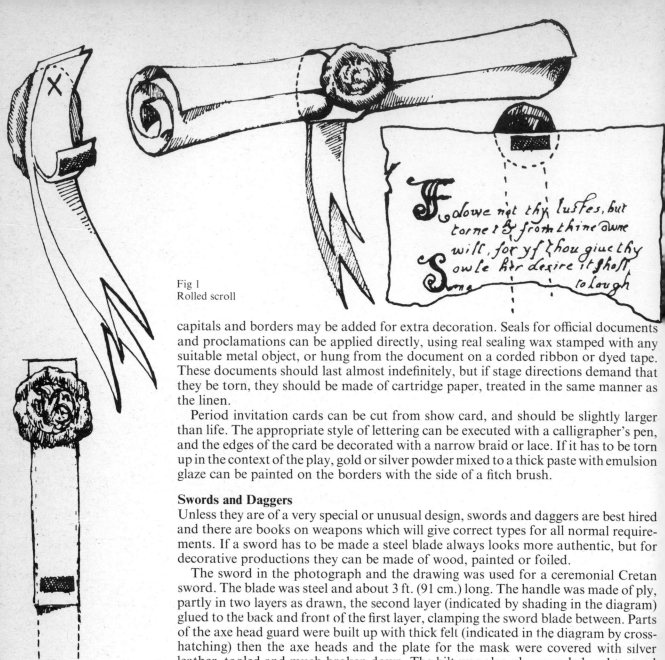

Fig 1
Rolled scroll

capitals and borders may be added for extra decoration. Seals for official documents and proclamations can be applied directly, using real sealing wax stamped with any suitable metal object, or hung from the document on a corded ribbon or dyed tape. These documents should last almost indefinitely, but if stage directions demand that they be torn, they should be made of cartridge paper, treated in the same manner as the linen.

Period invitation cards can be cut from show card, and should be slightly larger than life. The appropriate style of lettering can be executed with a calligrapher's pen, and the edges of the card be decorated with a narrow braid or lace. If it has to be torn up in the context of the play, gold or silver powder mixed to a thick paste with emulsion glaze can be painted on the borders with the side of a fitch brush.

Swords and Daggers

Unless they are of a very special or unusual design, swords and daggers are best hired and there are books on weapons which will give correct types for all normal requirements. If a sword has to be made a steel blade always looks more authentic, but for decorative productions they can be made of wood, painted or foiled.

The sword in the photograph and the drawing was used for a ceremonial Cretan sword. The blade was steel and about 3 ft. (91 cm.) long. The handle was made of ply, partly in two layers as drawn, the second layer (indicated by shading in the diagram) glued to the back and front of the first layer, clamping the sword blade between. Parts of the axe head guard were built up with thick felt (indicated in the diagram by cross-hatching) then the axe heads and the plate for the mask were covered with silver leather, tooled and much broken down. The hilt was also ply, rounded and tapered and bound with gold braid (glued to prevent slipping). Two wooden beads, painted black and rubbed with gold were set between the horns which formed the hilt, the bull's head was carved from polystyrene, scrimmed, painted dark gold and small pieces of coloured cinamoid were glued on to get the effect of mosaic.

The dagger illustrated was carved and turned out of wood and trimmed and decorated with velvet, braid, cords and wired out motifs.

Fabrics

Felt

Thick carpet felt, treated with soap, paint and shoe polish, makes an excellent substitute for leather, assuming that the real thing is either unobtainable or too expensive. Dampen a piece of yellow soap and rub it hard over the surface of the felt until it becomes shiny, leaving some rough patches. Scrub in some emulsion paint in a darker

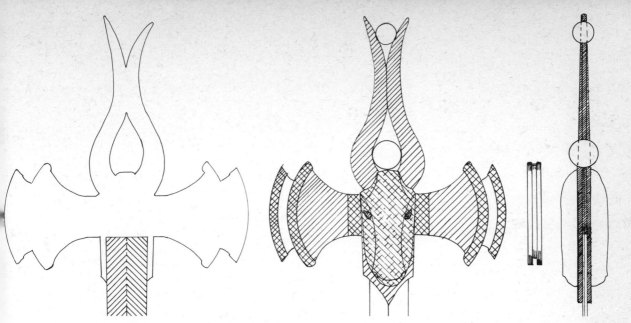

shade of the original felt colour and finally rub it over with brown or black shoe polish. Alternatively, the felt can be broken down in various shades of brown and black, then coated with polyvinyl. Both these treatments leave the felt flexible: if a hard leather is needed, size or resin should be used instead of polyvinyl or shoe polish.

Costume felt, which lends itself to stretching round awkward shapes, can be stuck on to a solid base with Copydex or an aerosol spray glue and coated when dry with a polyvinyl glaze. A wooden box can be covered in this way to give the appearance of a hide trunk. Cover the wooden base with a thin felt. Make corners and straps of thicker felt (these can be studded with upholstery studs if that finish is suitable). The dummy lock and clips can be made in thin ply, or thick felt treated with vinyl, and then decorated. Stick small pieces of felt or ply to the sides of the trunk where the handles are to be inserted and when these have dried bore through them and the sides of the trunk and insert rope for handles. For a buckskin or kid effect a white or off-white felt should be used, for a darker leather use a felt of suitable colour and paint over the glaze with F.E.V. in shades of brown and amber, darkening and ageing it round the handles and fastenings where it would have become worn.

A medium thickness of felt can be treated in the same way to make bags and knapsacks, but the prop should be made up first as sewing is difficult after the material has been treated.

Fig 2
Drawing showing construction of Cretan ceremonial sword

6 Sword and dagger

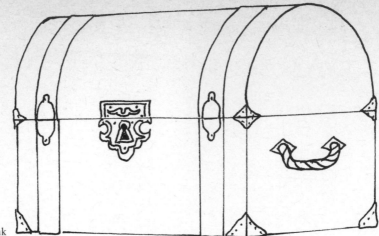

Fig 3
Hide trunk

For a drawstring-type purse, first cut a circular base, stiffened if that effect is wanted. Cut a strip of material the length of the circumference of the base, and cut slits in it for the drawstring. Stitch the strip into a cylinder, turn it inside out and stitch it to the base. Turn the whole thing the right way out and insert the drawstring.

A bag of the type illustrated in fig. 5 may be made as follows. Cut the top flap and back in one piece from felt or canvas which has been treated with vinyl, with a double thickness in a strip two thirds of the way up (indicated by shading in the diagram). Cut a front panel to match the back panel. Cut the side panel in one strip 2 or 3 in. (5 to 7·5 cm.) wide. Stitch the side panel to the back panel, rough stitching with button thread or fine string or thonging. Stitch the strap to the flap. Stitch the band for the strap to the front panel, then stitch the front panel to the side panel. If a shoulder bag is what's wanted, make the strap either from the same material as the bag or from carpet webbing, stitch two rings to the back of the bag with straps as shown, then slip the strap through the rings and stitch. Paint the whole bag with F.E.V. to represent leather.

Fig 4
Drawstring purse

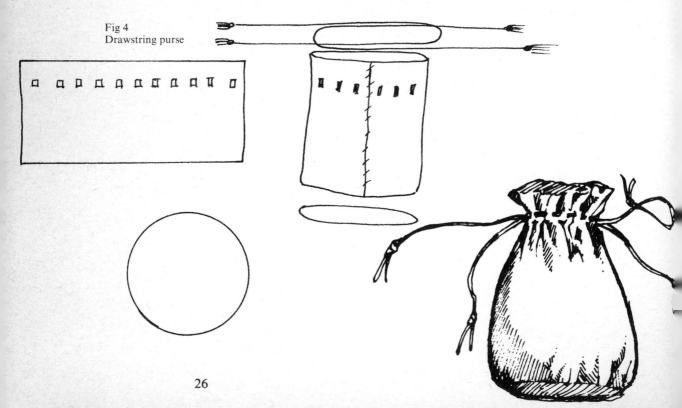

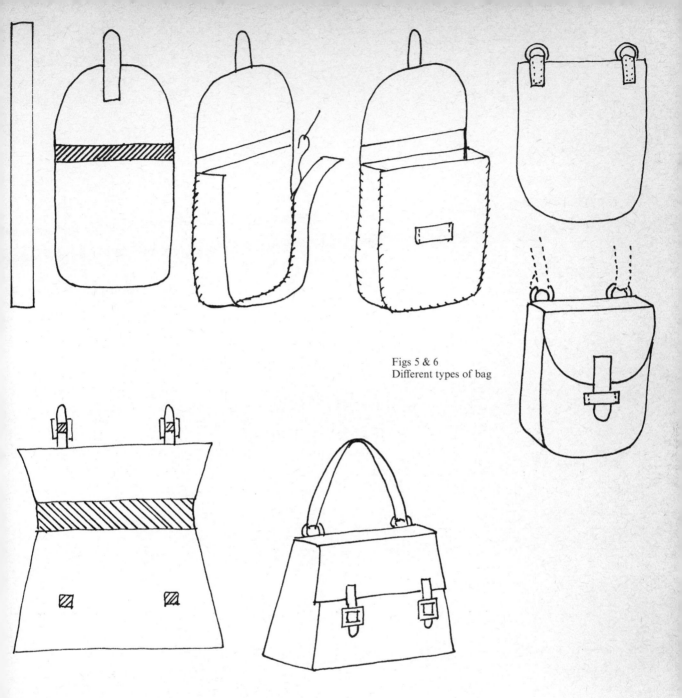

Figs 5 & 6
Different types of bag

The bag in fig. 6 is made in the same way but of course the pieces are cut in different shapes and it is fastened with dummy buckles. The buckles are fixed to the straps, which can then be stitched to the flap. Strips of Velcro are then stitched to the back of the straps, behind the buckles, and corresponding strips of Velcro are stitched to the front of the bag.

Tooled leather, on book covers for example, can be made by applying a very coarse lace under the felt. If a suitable lace is not available, a design could be cut in thin plywood or thick felt. After finishing, this tooling will need emphasizing with paint.

Felt always has a rough and rather shabby finish, however, and should not be used if the leather is to appear new. For new leather, use the real thing or a good plastic imitation.

Fig 7
'Wrought-iron' bracket

Thick carpet felts can also be used for making decorative carpets, if, as often happens, it is difficult to find or hire one of the size or design you require. Choose a suitable basic colour and cut it to shape. Then draw out the design in chalk or charcoal and paint it in scenic paint mixed with emulsion glaze. The edges of the carpet should be webbed to prevent it stretching out of shape and to make a firm edge for tacks if it is to be fixed to the stage. Scenic paint will give a good faded effect, but if you want a stronger colour it would be better to use a cheap felt and cover it with canvas or upholstery velour. This can be stuck, and, if necessary, sewn, down; the edges should be turned over and sewn down on the back. The design can then be painted on with dye, mixed with starch to prevent it running.

Black felt can be treated to give a convincing representation of iron work. Bands round chests and boxes, for example, can be made from strips of thick black felt coated, after they have been fixed in place, with size or resin. When they have hardened, a little silver paint can be dry-brushed on. A dummy lock can be made by cutting the shape in the same felt (or in plywood) and gluing it in place on the chest or door, inserting a few panel pins or wire nails for good measure. The felt can then be sized and painted and decorated with round-headed nails.

Wrought-iron work, used for a variety of decorative purposes in both interior and exterior settings, can also be constructed quite simply from black felt. Cut strips of thick black felt about 1 in. (2·5 cm.) wide and matching strips in thin black felt. Lay out all the strips on a flat surface and, using a spatula, cover them with a layer of Bostick or white glue like Elmer's. Place a wire of the appropriate length down the centre of each strip of thick felt and cover it with a strip of thin felt. Run your nails down each side of the enclosed wire, making sure that the felt is well bonded. Once the adhesive has set, twist the strips into shape. When assembling the work, fix the meeting points of the separate sections with Bostick (or with white glue), holding them with pegs or paper clips until it has set. The finished shape can be decorated with flowers, leaves, or other motifs, also cut from the felt and glued into place. Once the basic structure is complete, it should be brushed with resin. When this has set, and all temporary fixings have been removed, paint it with black F.E.V., adding a few highlights in gold or silver.

The same treatment can, of course, be applied to any iron implement. A spearhead, axe or pickaxe can be cut in ply, covered in black felt and finished as described above.

7 'Tooled leather' books with scrolls

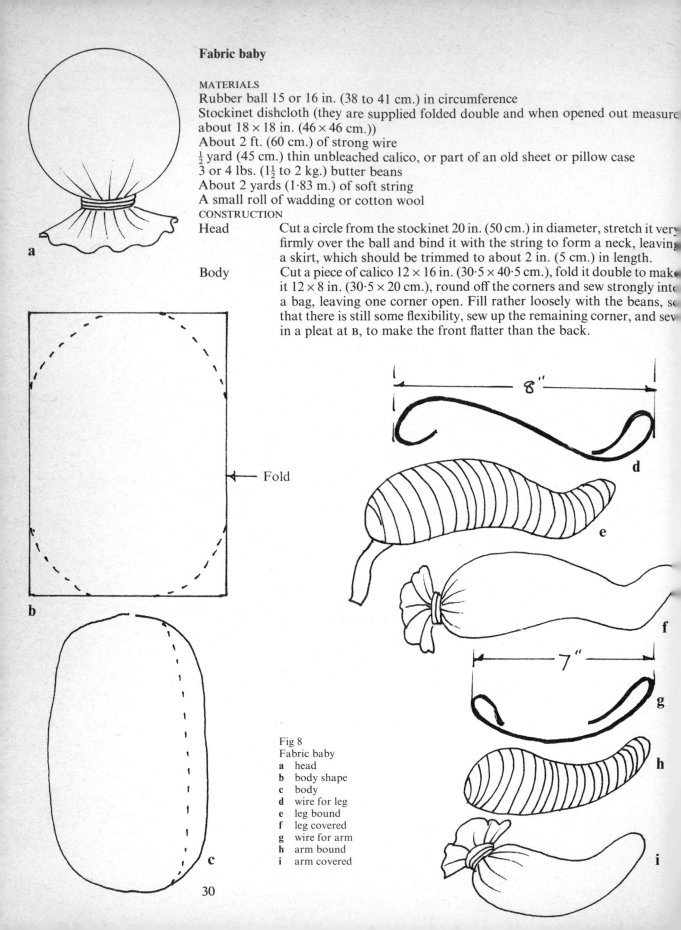

Fabric baby

MATERIALS

Rubber ball 15 or 16 in. (38 to 41 cm.) in circumference

Stockinet dishcloth (they are supplied folded double and when opened out measure about 18 × 18 in. (46 × 46 cm.))

About 2 ft. (60 cm.) of strong wire

½ yard (45 cm.) thin unbleached calico, or part of an old sheet or pillow case

3 or 4 lbs. (1½ to 2 kg.) butter beans

About 2 yards (1·83 m.) of soft string

A small roll of wadding or cotton wool

CONSTRUCTION

Head   Cut a circle from the stockinet 20 in. (50 cm.) in diameter, stretch it very firmly over the ball and bind it with the string to form a neck, leaving a skirt, which should be trimmed to about 2 in. (5 cm.) in length.

Body   Cut a piece of calico 12 × 16 in. (30·5 × 40·5 cm.), fold it double to make it 12 × 8 in. (30·5 × 20 cm.), round off the corners and sew strongly into a bag, leaving one corner open. Fill rather loosely with the beans, so that there is still some flexibility, sew up the remaining corner, and sew in a pleat at B, to make the front flatter than the back.

a

Fold

b

c

30

8"

d

e

f

7"

g

h

i

Fig 8
Fabric baby
a   head
b   body shape
c   body
d   wire for leg
e   leg bound
f   leg covered
g   wire for arm
h   arm bound
i   arm covered

Legs   Cut two pieces of wire 11 in. (28 cm.) long, and bend as in fig. 8d. The finished length should be 8 in. (20 cm.). Cut some thin strips of calico, pad the wire shapes with wadding or cotton wool and bind firmly with the calico strips until a good shape is obtained. Cut two pieces of stockinet 6 × 9 in. (15 × 23 cm.) with the stretch on the long way, fold into pieces 3 × 9 in. (7·5 × 23 cm.) and sew into bags open at one end. Pull these over the padded legs and tie off with string in the same way as the head.

Arms   Cut two pieces of wire 10 in. (25 cm.) long and bend as in fig. 8g. The finished length should be 7 in. (18 cm.). Bind on the wadding as for the legs. Cut two pieces of stockinet 5 × 6 in. (12·5 × 15 cm.), make into two bags 2½ × 6 in. (6·5 × 12·5 cm.), and proceed as for legs.

Assembly   Spread the skirt of the head over one end of the body, stretch it well and pin or tack it into place, leaving enough play to let the head move naturally. Sew it very strongly, and if the movement is still too much bind the neck with more string. Fix the legs and arms in the same way to the outside edges of the body near the rounded corners, leaving a natural amount of movement.

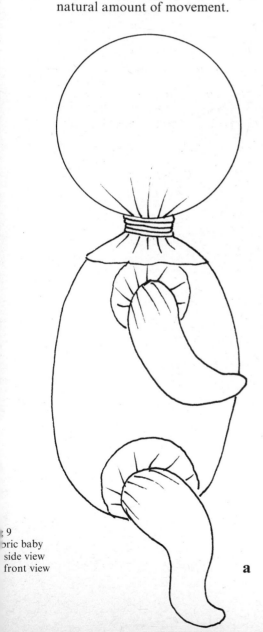

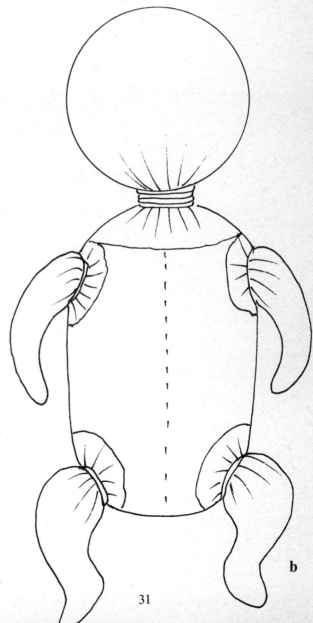

9
Fabric baby
side view
front view

a

b

Fig 10
Bird wing and tail

Fabric birds and animals

While dead birds or animals are most frequently called for, there are also occasion
when a dummy must be substituted for a live creature in order to avoid distractin
noise or movement on stage. Always work from a good reference picture, or, bette
still, make working drawings from a study of the live subject, if necessary in a zoo c
an aviary.

Whether the creature is dead or alive, the basic working process is the same.

Using a paper pattern, cut the two halves of the body shape from calico or thin fel
using a flesh colour in case it shows. Sew the two sections together, leaving gaps fc
inserting the stuffing. Fill quite solidly with Dacron wadding or lima beans. The hea
should be carved in polystyrene or wood and weighted, if necessary, with lead dre
weights. It can then be attached to a tubular neck, stuffed very loosely. The process s
far described can be used for both birds and animals.

Next, in the case of birds, make the wings and tail. Cut the basic shapes in stiff nylc
net and add extra thickness on the wings where the bones would be; this can be dor
with layers of felt or buckram (indicated in the diagram by shading). The wings ca
then be feathered. If possible, use real flight feathers of a suitable colour and sew the
into place at the flight end of the wings. For the rest of the wing, feather pads (whic
are available from milliners' suppliers) can be used. Stick them down with Bostic
(white glue), overlapping them all the way to the bone end. The completed wings ca
be stitched to the body with a flap so that they are flexible. Feather the tail in the san
way and stitch it to the body. The head and neck should now be stitched on. Mal
the legs and feet from wire, padding and feathering the thighs and binding the shanl

32

with felt or calico. Attach them to the body. Now feather the whole bird with feather pads, starting at the tail end, and overlapping them all the way to the head, for which a few separate small feathers will be needed. Sequin or bead eyes can then be stuck on and the beak and legs painted. If real feathers are not available, cut the appropriate shapes from thin felt, velvet or other suitable fabric and layer them over each other. They will, of course, have to be painted from a good reference.

For animals, after the body has been made and stuffed, the head carved and fixed to a neck, the legs must be made. First make an armature of ply, jointed rather like the limbs of a wooden doll. Pad them and bind them with calico or cover them with stockinet. Man-made furs are now almost indistinguishable from the real thing, so choose one which is suitable. Cover the legs and then sew them to the body by flaps in the same way as the bird wings. Now attach the head and neck and cover them and the body with the fur. Ears, eyes, tail, and claws or hooves should then be added. (All except the feet should be attached loosely, so that they are not too rigid.) Again, if fur is too expensive, painted felt or velvet can substitute, especially for short-haired animals.

This method can be adapted to make a variety of creatures; most in demand, however, are rabbits and hares, chickens, ducks and geese. If the animals are really big, like stags, for instance, the body will have to be carved from polystyrene and some weight set into it. Real horns and glass eyes can be used. It can be covered with upholstery velvet which makes a very good hide when painted and broken down.

8 Sacrificial bird from *Idomeneo*, Sadler's Wells Theatre, 1962. Photo: Donald Southern

Banners

The problem of weight must be considered in the case of very big banners attached to long poles. They will be easy to carry if lightweight aluminium tubes, 1½ in. to 2 in. (3·8 cm. to 5 cm.) in diameter are used for the poles. They can be painted with oil paint to look like wood, or treated with gold or silver foil, broken down with F.E.V. If stage directions demand the waving of a flag the best fabric to use is Jap silk as it is light and floats well. The design can be appliquéd with a heavier silk or a thin felt or it can be painted on with fabric inks or paints. A lightweight fringe can be sewn round the edge. For very large ceremonial or battle standards it is better to use tapestry canvas, painted with a thin solution of scenic paint mixed with emulsion medium. This fabric is rather stiff and does not hang so limply as a soft material; it looks more alive and as if the wind is in it. A heavier cotton or metal bullion fringe can be sewn to these. For methods of fixing banners and standards to their staffs see the diagrams.

To create the effect of shelled or battle-torn standards lay the finished standard flat on the floor and cut out the 'shell' holes. Fine black net should be stuck on behind the holes to fill them and prevent further tearing. The edges of the holes should be ragged, and blackened with paint to represent scorching. Battle and mud stains can be added at this stage, by spattering from a broad scene painters' brush. This is done by holding a broom handle or pole rigidly in one hand and after dipping the brush into the paint, striking the flat side of the handle very smartly against the stick. This gives a spotted or spattered appearance, rather than a trailed one, as happens when the brush is not stopped sharply. The fringed edges should be tattered and some parts left hanging, or removed altogether. The torn and battered effect can also be obtained by well-controlled burning.

9 *The Master Singers*, London Coliseum, 1974. Photo: Anthony Crickmay. Banners made from painted embroidery canvas

Fig 11
Fixing the banner to the pole
a dowel and finial
b banner with pocket for pole.
   Shaded sections are cut out
c cord is fixed to completed
   banner at A. When slipped
   over the finial it keeps the
   banner from sliding down the
   pole

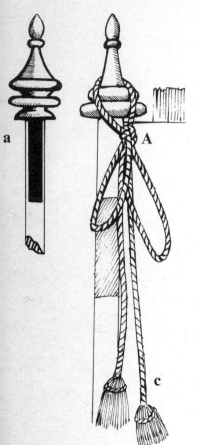

10 Battle-worn French standard,
made from embroidery canvas.
Used in the London Coliseum
production of *War and Peace*,
1973. Photo: Donald Southern

11 Construction of urn in process. Photo: Donald Southern

Fibreglass and papier-mâché

Large pottery vessels can be made quite inexpensively from chicken wire and wooden formers finished either with fibreglass or papier-mâché.

Working method

First make a scale drawing showing the sizes and positions of the wooden formers. Enlarge the scale to full size, scribe the shapes out on $\frac{3}{8}$ in. (1 cm.) ply and then cut them out, removing the centres to lessen the final weight, but leaving the base solid for stability. Then link the cut shapes with narrow strips of skin ply, countersinking them into the edges. With tin snips cut several manageable strips of chicken wire and, starting from the base, nail them to the rims of the formers with $\frac{3}{4}$ in. (2 cm.) gimp pins, bending over the heads to hold the wire. The chicken wire may have to be pinched in or stretched to fit according to the width of the former. Continue this process until the whole vessel is formed. If any gaps are left in the wire, cut extra pieces and lace them

37

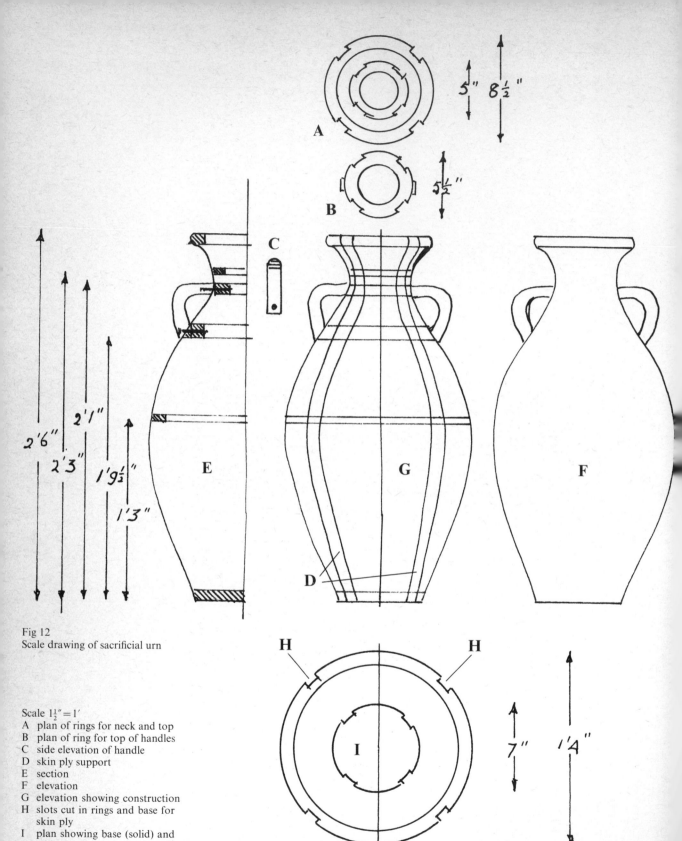

Fig 12
Scale drawing of sacrificial urn

Scale $1\frac{1}{2}'' = 1'$
A plan of rings for neck and top
B plan of ring for top of handles
C side elevation of handle
D skin ply support
E section
F elevation
G elevation showing construction
H slots cut in rings and base for
   skin ply
I plan showing base (solid) and
   widest ring

12 Completed urn. Photo: John Poulter

in by means of their own rough edges. Cover the frame with fibreglass in the following way. First cut the matting into squares. Pour about half a pint ($\frac{1}{4}$ litre) of resin into a polythene bowl, add about a teaspoonful of catalyst and mix it thoroughly. Finally add three or four drops of hardener. You must work fast as it only takes a matter of minutes for it to congeal. Apply the squares of matting to the framework with a brush full of resin, overlapping them and making sure they are saturated. (Brushes must be cleaned afterwards with the appropriate solvent.) If fibreglass is too expensive or complicated the old papier-mâché method is also suitable but it takes longer both to do and to dry. First the wire framework must be scrimmed to form a good solid base for the paper. Tear sheets of blue and grey sugar paper into irregular sized pieces and soak them in water, each colour in a separate container, until they are soft and pliable. Mix some Polycell paste (as directed on the packet) and paint an area of the scrimmed netting with it. Then, with the same paste-filled brush, stick on the blue sugar paper pieces, overlapping them and working the paste well in. When the first layer has dried, apply the second layer, using the grey paper. The two different colours allow a visual check that there are no gaps in the second layer. When the piece has dried out, uneven surfaces must be sandpapered down. It may even be advisable to apply a butter muslin scrimming, to make a good surface for painting. Both fibreglass and papier-mâché vessels can be painted with scenic colour in a strong emulsion medium, that is to say, not much diluted. The designs can be painted either with acrylics or with F.E.V. A glaze can be applied if it is appropriate for the type of pottery represented.

Polystyrene and foam plastic

A wide variety of extremely convincing but totally inedible foodstuffs can be fashioned from these two materials. Anything from a royal banquet to a crust of bread may be needed, and my own experience in opera covers dishes ranging from roast sucking pig, with a section already cut out to show the ribs, to a roast peacock dressed all over in feathers and with tail in full display. The head of this bird had to be wrenched off during each performance, and this was achieved by stitching Velcro to the underside of the severed head and to the top surface of the neck, which was still attached to the body; the join was made invisible by overlapping feathers. Another opera required a procession of flunkeys carrying silver salvers: one held a roast iguana set in a bed of sliced bananas and garnished with paw-paws, another a lobster in a bed of rice, surrounded by oysters and shrimps, and yet another a boar's head with all the pipings and trimmings, down to a lemon in the mouth. The basic shapes for all the big objects were carved out of polystyrene, which was then scrimmed and painted or dressed with real feathers. The success of such props depends on good carving and painting.

Fish seems to be a popular stage dish, whether half-eaten or freshly caught. Foam plastic is the best material for making fish. Cut it in a good basic shape, with the head and tail separate if it has to appear flexible. The one illustrated was supposed to be fresh, so it had to be flexible. It was entirely made from foam plastic. The head was made separately from the body and joined loosely afterwards, using the outer skin to overlap the join. An incision was cut in the centre of the head at the gill end and a 2 in. (5 cm.) strip of carpet binding inserted, leaving the end projecting to be inserted in a similar incision in the body (6007 glue, which is specially made for binding foam plastic, was used for this, and Scotch Contact would also be suitable). The head end of the main body was cut very thin to fit in the incision cut in the gills and an incision was cut in this end to take the piece of binding left projecting from the head. The tail was made of pieces of foam plastic, glued, slightly spaced, on a strip of carpet webbing. It was weighted at the end by sewing in dress weights, until the correct action was decided upon. The plastic fish was then covered with silver lurex, using nylon net to make the fins and tail. Incisions were cut to represent the gills, and the eyes were made from pearl sequins, with a smaller black one superimposed for the pupil.

Both polystyrene and foam plastic are ideal for cakes and desserts. They are easy

to model: all you need is a sharp, long-bladed knife, surform and glasspaper (sand-paper) for cakes and sharp scissors and a knife for the other dishes. Small items such as savouries or buns can be cut direct from either substance and for sponge cakes or pastry add decoration (real glacé cherries, angelica, etc.). Careful and imaginative painting is essential for a realistic appearance. Tiered wedding cakes and other iced confectionery are improved by applying Polyfilla with a spatula over the basic shape and then painting with white emulsion. This looks very like frosted icing. Piping and decoration can be represented by fine piping cord, nylon crin, and silver braids and laces. You can also use real crystallized violet or rose petals, angelica and silver balls.

13 Model of roast iguana. Photo: John Poulter

14 Model of large, freshly caught fish. Photo: Donald Southern

41

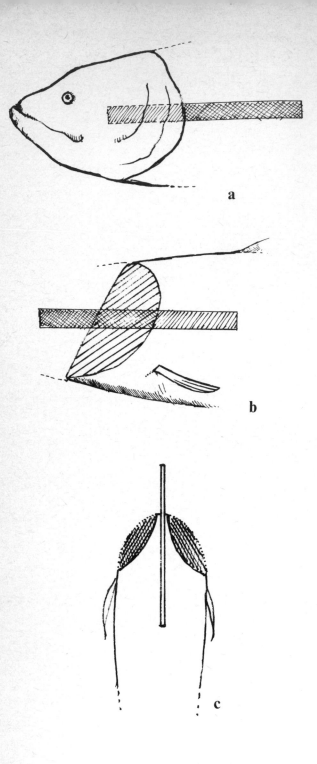

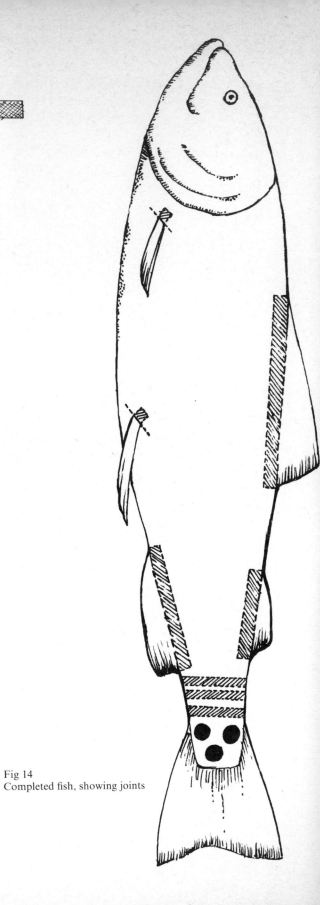

Fig 13
Details for making fish
a head with strip of carpet binding
b binding inserted into body, side view
c binding inserted into body, top view

Fig 14
Completed fish, showing joints

42

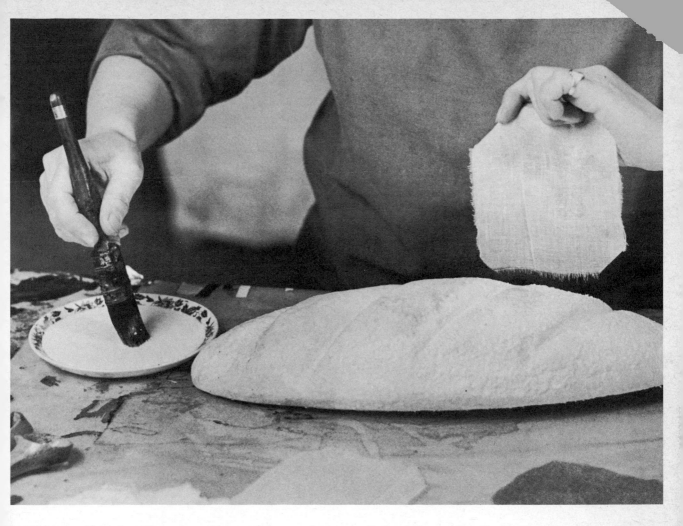

All kinds of bread and loaves can be carved from polystyrene. It should be scrimmed with butter muslin and coated with white emulsion. When dry, paint over it with a very diluted solution of F.E.V., as near to light basic bread colour as possible, leaving a few doughy patches. Finally add golden brown crust colours. For a top floury effect, dry brush on some white emulsion.

Poultry and game birds need scrimming after they have been carved from polystyrene. They should then be given an undercoat of emulsion, before being finally painted and glazed. Good cookery books will have diagrams of trussed birds, explanations of how to use real feathers for dressing and illustrations of suitable garnishings.

15 Scrimming a loaf of bread.
Photo: John Garner

Moulding and Casting

ROGER OLDHAMSTEAD

Busts, statues, and other cast objects are certain to be called for from time to time and in order to produce these the property maker must acquire some knowledge of moulding and casting. Unless he has talent, however, he will have to restrict himself to modelling simple objects, tackling more difficult pieces by making moulds and casts of existing objects and building up on them. For large sculptures, figures, portrait busts and masks he may have to enlist the help of a sculptor, as the modelling of figures and heads is usually beyond the range of anyone who has not had training and experience. Such things as a series of book backs, ornaments and formal details in architecture and furniture should be within the scope of a good prop maker.

Modelling

Plasticine and modelling clay, either plain or the plasticized variety which does not dry out so quickly, are ideal to model with and easy to cast from. When building up a shape that is going to be cast, it is important to remember not to undercut the modelling, i.e. as a general rule, the widest part of the shape should be on the modelling board and there should be no pieces overhanging or protruding that would create problems in casting.

Moulds

Moulds, of course, have sometimes to be made from complicated sculptures, and they have to be made in several pieces. Experience should be gained first with simple shapes. Making a two-part mould is described in the section on Special and Trick Props. An examination of any object that has been cast will show very clearly the seam lines in the mould; plastic dolls, cheap china and reproductions of sculpture, will all give the would-be mould maker a clear idea of how to set about dividing an object for making moulds for himself.

Moulds can be made from: plaster of paris, Vinamould, silicon rubber, flexible dental plaster, latex rubber, and plaster scrim. The methods of using these materials are described in the following pages.

Plaster of paris

This is the quickest, cheapest and most easily handled of moulding materials. It is only suitable, however, for moulding objects which can lie flat and are not more than about 6 in. (15 cm.) deep, since it is viscous and takes about ten minutes to solidify. Nor, because it is so brittle when set, can it be used for repeated castings.

Place the object to be moulded on a greased board and build a low clay or plasticine wall, leaving about a 2 in. (5 cm.) clearance all round it to prevent the plaster from spreading. Then treat the object with a releasing agent, such as vaseline, soap or petroleum jelly. Next, mix the plaster: for an average sized mask, for instance, put about one pint of cold water in a bowl, and sprinkle plaster into it until it will not absorb any more and the plaster begins to float on the top. Then mix it gently, kneading out all the lumps. As soon as it is smooth, pour it carefully to avoid making air bubbles, over the object, which should be well covered (to a thickness of at least 1 in. (2·5 cm.) over the most prominent part). The mould can be removed when it has hardened thoroughly. Provided there is no undercutting, not too much elaborate decoration, and the object is not porous, the mould thus made will provide a limited number of casts, without a great deal of preparation.

Plaster of paris can be used for making life masks, but this is rather a tricky operation and first attempts should be made under expert supervision. Careful precautions must be taken to prevent the plaster from spreading or sticking to the skin, hair and eyebrows. Straws must be inserted in the nostrils to allow the subject to breathe. Having a life mask made is quite an unpleasant experience and some people are apt to panic when they feel the weight of the plaster and when their eyes and mouth are covered, the only contact with the air being through the straws in their nose. Besides this the plaster warms up considerably as it sets and contracts slightly, all of which is quite uncomfortable, but the 'patient' does get a cast of his face as compensation.

Before making a cast the inside of the mould must be well coated with a release agent. Excellent and time consuming modelling jobs have been wasted because of an inadequately treated mould that ended up firmly attached to its cast.

Vinamould

A flexible, self-releasing moulding compound that is heated in a double boiler to a liquid state and poured on the object to be cast, which, because the substance is liquid and hot, must be in a heatproof container such as a tobacco or biscuit tin which can be sealed. This material can be re-heated and re-used several times and is therefore very suitable for small props, such as medallions, bosses and decorative motifs, when money is limited. Drying time is according to the thickness of the mould, approximately one hour per inch of thickness, and it is better to leave it overnight. Vinamould does allow a limited amount of undercutting.

Silicon rubber

This is the most expensive and sophisticated of moulding compounds. It is set by a catalyst, which is provided with the products, and forms a permanent, flexible, heatproof, self-releasing mould, which will take a certain amount of undercutting and produces a high definition surface that does not deteriorate even after making hundreds of casts. It is therefore very suitable for large runs of goblets, armour, shields, relief panels, sculpture, in fact anything requiring many copies, or with elaborate surface modelling. It combines strength with easy release from the mould.

All the above materials can be obtained from artists' or sculptors' suppliers and more information about usage and techniques is available with the products.

Flexible dental plaster

This is desirable for painless life masks, when faithful reproduction of skin texture is wanted. This material, like silicon rubber, is expensive and it has to be obtained from dental suppliers. Its drawback is that it has a short life and the cast must be taken within twelve hours of making the mould, after which time it ceases to be flexible. When making a life mask of this material it is not necessary to use painful straws in the victim's' nose, nor does it heat up as it sets as does ordinary plaster. As it is of a putty like consistency the whole face may be covered, with the exception of the nostrils. The plaster should be applied with a spatula, and mixed in small quantities as it sets rapidly. The face should be greased with petroleum jelly to prevent any possibility of

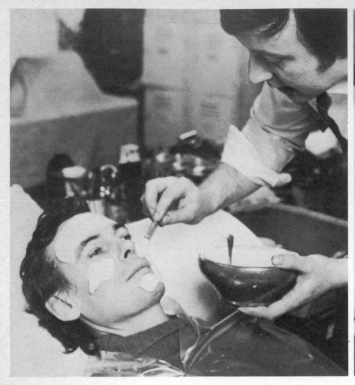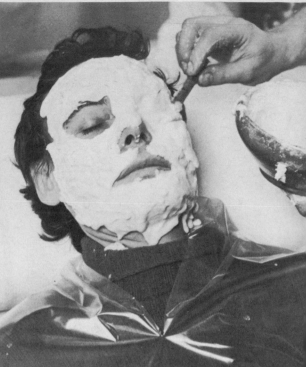

16 Starting to make a life mask of flexible dental plaster

17 Covering the eyes

18 Covering the mouth; the nostrils of course, must never be covered

19 Removing the mould from the face

Photos: John Garner

the mould sticking to the eyebrows or skin hair. N.B. A life mask should never be attempted, in any moulding compound, from anyone with a beard, moustache or side burns as even if the hair is well soaped down it is impossible to guarantee that the mould can be removed.

When the completed mould has been removed, it can be sealed with shellac or resin and a cast made from latex or papier-mâché. Or, if a model of the whole head is required, it can be filled at once with plaster of paris to make a positive of the face, the back can be modelled with clay or plasticine, and the whole thing recast in two pieces with plaster of paris, or one of the other mould making materials. Flexible dental plaster can, of course, be used for moulding anything which requires a very detailed and accurate mould, but as it is so expensive it is better to avoid it unless it is considered necessary.

Latex rubber
This is a safe material, requiring no particular precautions. It is particularly useful for anything which needs to be flexible or which is hard or sharp or might break easily. It is ammonia based and vulcanizes on contact with the air. It may be used to make a mould by painting the object with the rubber, and allowing it to dry, forming a skin. The process should be repeated several times, and every second layer reinforced with muslin or scrim (cut in small pieces) for strength. The mould must then be left, on the subject, for two or three days in a warm place, then carefully removed and cleaned in soap and water. Before casting from a latex rubber mould it must be treated either with soap or a manufactured release agent but not oil, as this attacks the rubber.

Plaster scrim
This can be used as a quick or 'one-off' method of mould making. The scrim bandage impregnated with plaster of paris, the type used for setting broken bones, is hardened by dipping in water. Two or three minutes is the usual setting time, so only a small quantity should be dipped at a time. This is also a good safe method of making life masks as it is easily controllable and is moderately comfortable for the wearer. It can

20 A plaster mould made in two parts and a cast made with latex rubber 'skin'

46

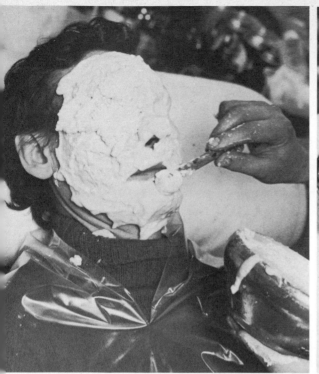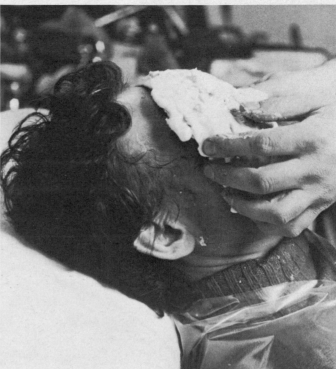

also be used directly over wire mesh to make rough-surfaced objects, such as logs or tree trunks. It can be bought from a chemist's shop or pharmacy.

Casts and finishes

Casts can be made from the following: plaster of paris and plaster scrim; latex rubber and casting foam; papier-mâché; scrim or muslin plus glue; polyester resins and glass fibre matting.

Plaster of paris

Plaster casts are brittle and not suitable for pieces that are going to be handled or moved, but for a 'one-off' performance they are adequate, and plaster is one of the cheapest casting materials.

To make a cast from plaster. When the mould is completely set and hard, check it for any flaws or air bubbles. If you find any, fill them carefully with plasticine or clay. Then, if necessary, coat the inside of the mould with a release agent. Mix the plaster as described above and pour it carefully into the mould. When it is thoroughly set take it out for finishing. If the mould is also of plaster it may not be possible to remove it in one piece, as there is a lot of suction, but if you proceed gently, taking care not to damage the cast, this is not too serious as you will still have the cast. If the surface is not as smooth as you could wish, rub it down gently with very fine glass or sandpaper, repeating the process until you are satisfied.

Plaster does not take paint too readily, but, if it is first primed with shellac, paint with an emulsion medium or acrylics should give satisfactory results.

Latex rubber

Latex is often used for masks which are to be worn, and for other applications where flexibility, lightness, or safety are important. Axe blades, daggers, clubs, chains, bottles, for example, can all be cast in latex from moulds. Paint the mould sections with latex and allow them to dry. Repeat this process two or three times, reinforcing every other layer with muslin or scrim to prevent tearing, until the required thickness is built up. Join separate sections of the cast by painting latex on to the edges, and pushing them together when the latex is tacky.

All latex casts must be allowed to cure for two or three days in a warm room before painting, as they are liable to distort or dry out of shape if handled too early.

Latex rubber may also be used as a paint, to strengthen fabrics or to keep felt or other fabric in shape when used for items such as body armour, or to put a non-slip back on carpets and rugs.

Certain metal-based paints have a harmful effect on latex; it is therefore advisable to give the cast a coating of emulsion medium, water-based paint or acrylic medium before the finishing coat, which can then be of almost any kind of paint, except F.E.

An important use for latex rubber is for mouldings and cornices on scenery. Accidental knocks and scuffs will do far less damage to this material than to poly styrene or even wood. The heaviest grade of rubber available should be used, and a good deal of reinforcement must be incorporated.

Casting foam

A special type of cast used for life masks is made with casting foam in a latex-lined mould. The method is described fully in the section on Special Props.

Papier-mâché

Either sugar paper or newspaper can be used for this old-fashioned way of making casts. Tear the paper into small pieces (not more than 2 in. (5 cm.) square) and soak them in water. Treat the mould with a release agent, petroleum jelly or soap. Then, using Polycell or a cold water paste, work the paper into the mould with a paste-filled brush, making sure that it is well pressed down and that there are no paste or air bubbles. Paste a layer of shredded scrim or butter muslin between each paper layer

48

When using sugar paper it is useful to use blue paper for the first layer and grey for the second, and so on. This allows a visual check that each layer is a complete cover. Remove the cast from the mould and when it has completely dried out rub it down gently with glasspaper (emery cloth). Coat it with shellac and, when this is dry, apply a coat of emulsion paint. If a very smooth surface is wanted it can be smoothed again with the glasspaper and given another coat of paint. This process should be repeated until a perfect surface is obtained.

This is the cheapest way of making a cast and, with careful treatment, it should last reasonably well.

Scrim or muslin plus glue

The working method is the same as for papier-mâché, but fabric is used instead of paper and Scotch glue instead of Polycell or cold water paste. It makes a very light, translucent object, but it is not as durable as papier-mâché.

Polyester resins

These resins should be used with extreme caution. Work only in well ventilated rooms, use a mask to prevent the inhalation of particles (masks with replacement pads can be bought very cheaply from a chemist's shop or paint store) and avoid getting resin on the skin.

Instructions for the quantities of resin and catalyst are printed on the containers and must be followed. The catalyst organic peroxide is a corrosive, toxic substance and should, as all chemicals, be treated with respect.

To cast in resin, first prepare the mould with a release agent. Then apply a gel or skin with thickened (thixotropic) resin to fill in some of the fine detail. Allow this to set and, if the mould is very large, repeat the process. Then apply one or more layers of fibreglass matting with ordinary polyester resin. When it is thoroughly set pull the cast carefully out of the mould and wash off the release agent with warm water and soap. The cast is now ready for painting. Resin will take any kind of paint, including F.E.V., oils, emulsion or acrylics.

It is suggested that one of the many books on polyester resins be consulted before they are used, as the subject is too complicated for an exhaustive explanation to be given here.

They are particularly useful for work in the theatre because of their speed of casting, lightness and strength (for weight and permanence), and because waterproof and fire resistant finishes are available.

Large panels or screens, for example, can be constructed with maximum speed and the framework can be cut to the minimum. Panels of, say, 4×4 ft. ($1 \cdot 2 \times 1 \cdot 2$ m.) can be modelled and moulded, then cast with resin reinforced with fibreglass matting. Several casts from the same mould can be joined to form larger panels and only require a very light wood or metal framework. They are much less heavy than conventional plywood constructions and much more durable than polystyrene. Resin can also be used for casting other large items such as armour (breast plates, helmets, swords, etc.), statuary, busts, relief panels, small rostrums, rocks, boxes, steps, urns, large containers and tubs, trees, doors and mouldings, and smaller items including jewellery, small vases and ornaments, goblets, jugs, and face masks, if they are suitably lined.

Interesting texture and colour finishes can be made by adding substances to the resin before casting. There are special polyester resin pigments which come in very brilliant clear colours and do not affect the setting of the resin. For quite a brilliant metal finish, with more shine than metal paints, metallic powders can be added. Whiting (obtainable from paint dealers) when added to the resin gives a marble-like effect and the addition of graphite or slate powder will give the resin the appearance of stone. Sawdust can be added, either by itself or in conjunction with any of the other substances, to give a rough surface texture.

Apart from their use for casting, polyester resins can be used to harden felt, to seal

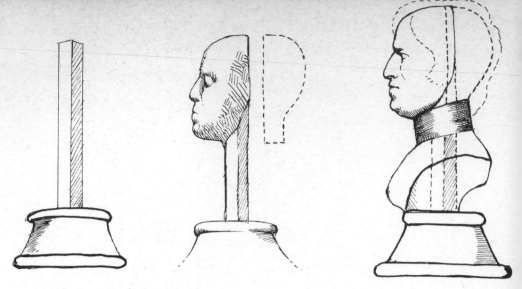

Fig 15
Details of portrait bust

and harden surfaces such as soft wood and to solidify rope, lace and drapery.

All these applications are illustrated in the sculptures made for two recent productions of the English National Opera, the portrait busts for *War and Peace* and the Spanish Madonna for *Il Trovatore:* the making of these is given in detail below.

For the portrait busts, a turned wood plinth was made from hardwood (the plinth would have been less expensive if it had been designed square). A wooden framework was then set into this, to which the face, which had already been modelled, and cast in reinforced resin, was added. The back of the head, shoulders, chest and back were constructed in chicken wire, the neck being formed of a suitably sized cardboard tube. This form was then covered in resin reinforced with fibreglass matting. It was applied with a brush, in even layers, forming the shape of the shoulders and chest. The bust was then ready for decoration. The hair was formed from paper rope, although it could have been made from strips of felt dipped in resin. (In making sculpture of this kind it is necessary to use a period reference for the arrangement of the hair and as a general identification of style. It is important to get period flavour into sculpture as it sets the mood and atmosphere on the stage and is virtually another member of the cast.) The uniform coats and collars were cut out of stiff felt $\frac{1}{4}$ in. (0·66 cm.) thick. The pieces were sewn together and fitted on the figure as on a tailor's dummy. They were then removed, dipped in resin, put back on the figure and pinned into place. Some rather expensive French lace was used to decorate the collars and facings of the uniform and this was pinned into place after being soaked in resin. The drape was made of soft grade felt, dipped in resin and fixed into place, while wet, with pins or nails. It was necessary to experiment with the dry fabric first for shape and position, as the resin sets rapidly.

The finish was very important. As it was to be marble, an off-white ground, scenic paint with emulsion medium, was applied. Then a coat of Vandyke crystals, well diluted with water, was painted all over with a large brush, and wiped off at once with a cloth, leaving 'dirt' in the cracks and the moulding. A final highlight in a paler tone than the off-white ground was added to prominent surfaces, to give extra life to the modelling. It is essential to break down and accentuate shadows even in relief or modelled work, as stage lighting cancels out so much.

The Spanish Madonna was an example of freer sculpture, using all the above methods. The only casts were of the face and hands. The shape was built up over a wooden frame and the costume made in resin-stiffened felt, with decorations in real lace, wood, plastic, felt, fringe and pearls; the lace handkerchief and jewellery stones were added afterwards. The gold crown and nimbus were cut from plywood, in layers, textured in gold resin and then given a coat of Dutch metal (imitation gold leaf) applied with adhesive. The completed figure was painted in bright scarlet and blue

21 Two portrait busts from the London Coliseum production of *War and Peace*, 1973. Photo: Donald Southern

22 Spanish Madonna used in the London Coliseum production of *Il Trovatore*, 1973. Photo: Donald Southern

with black, white and gold (scene paint with emulsion medium), then covered in Vandyke brown water dye and rubbed off with a cloth to simulate worn wood. Final additions of amber glass stones, crystal tears, false eyelashes and a white dove completed the figure, which stands nearly nine feet (2·75 m.) high.

    Instead of resin, for all except the casting of faces and hands, it would have been quite possible to use Scotch glue as a much cheaper alternative. But where speed is required and certainty of setting time is essential resin is more satisfactory.

Points to remember when using resin are:
1   It sets rapidly, so work out exactly what you are going to do before you start.
2   It will need reinforcing for strength as by itself it tends to be somewhat brittle: fibreglass matting is a good reinforcement.
3   It eats into polystyrene and certain foam plastics, so cover them in metal foil first to protect them.

It is impossible to give a rigid set of rules for materials and method as prop making is a continuous process of improvisation and experiment, with many new materials being added to the list every year. The real test of a good prop is its practicability, finish, weight and the sureness with which it has been executed. A beautiful mould is never going to appear on the stage, only the cast, and if this is badly finished or carelessly painted, then no amount of technical knowledge will compensate.

23   Moulded helmets and armour in *Coriolanus*, the RSC production at the Aldwych Theatre, 1973. Photo: Douglas Jeffrey

24 Casket made of plywood and
moulded latex rubber, painted
with metallic gold in *The
Merchant of Venice*, the RSC
production at the Aldwych
Theatre, 1972. Photo: Philip Sayer

25 Fibre glass resin statue in
Carving a Statue, Haymarket
Theatre, 1964. Photo: Angus
McBean

Light Fittings and Fires

ROGER OLDHAMSTEAD

Most productions need some sort of light fittings, whether oil, candles, gas or electric. They may be practical or simply decorative. They should, basically, be provided by the electrical department, who are responsible for the wiring, lamp fittings and plugging up. The prop maker is responsible for dressing the basic structure provided by the electrics.

Real lamps and chandeliers are too dangerous to use on stage and would be expensive to replace if they got broken. Fortunately there are many plastic alternatives to glass which are cheaper, safer and almost as effective.

Live flames, of course, are hardly ever possible on stage as fire precautions are very strict, but if a lighted candle can be proved to be essential to the action of the play, and if it is in the charge of an actor throughout, permission for it is sometimes granted.

Chandeliers

Frames can be made, to a design, by a carpenter or metal worker. They must then be wired and the lamp holders fitted by the electrical department, before any decoration is added. The one in the photograph here is constructed from six sections of metal strip, bent to shape and bolted to a six-sided central post, which has a hanging ring at the top. The 'cut glass' cups are plexiglas sugar bowls drilled out at the centre to take the 1-in. (2·5 cm.) cardboard sleeves (representing the candles) for the electrical fittings, which are fixed on short metal rods, bolted in an upright position. The flower and foliage decorations are bought plastic goods, painted flat white, then sprayed with gold. These were wired on to the frames which were then broken down with brown F.E.V. to give a slight patina. The 'glass' balls at the base are simply plastic bowls glued together and attached by wire to a ring at the base of the post. The tear-shaped glass drops are bought plastic pieces, added to give a little sparkle to the finished chandelier, which otherwise would appear as gilded metal. The measurements are approximately 6×7 ft. ($1·83 \times 2·13$ m.) to the ball. This is fairly standard size, and quite often larger ones are required.

The branch chandelier in the line drawing is practical, and so the central column and scrolls had to be made of metal tubing. If it is only required to be decorative they can be cane. The candles and holders are cardboard tubing, and the drip pans are tin lids supported by thin strips of metal. Small rubber balls can be cut and fitted over the tubing for decoration.

Oil lamps

Nineteenth-century oil lamps are rather complex in shape and mechanism, so it is often more satisfactory to hire or buy them. Oil lamps always, of course, have a

26 The chandelier from the
London Coliseum production of
A Masked Ball, 1965. Photo: Reg
Wilson

Fig 16
Simple four-branch chandelier
a   elevation
b   ceiling discs decorated with
    paper rope
c   plan of drip tray
d   plan of construction
e   section showing wiring and
    tubular casing
f   detail of candle and drip tray

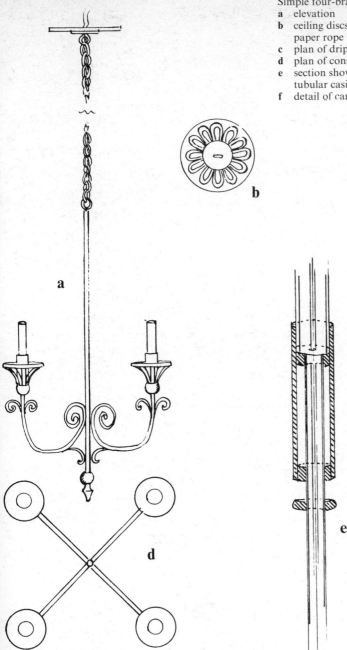

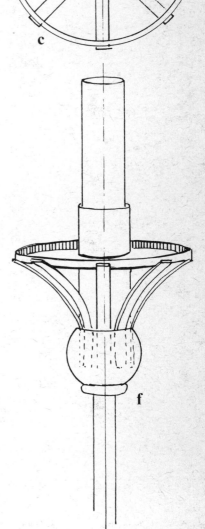

container for the oil. They also have a collar and winders for the wicks, combined with a gallery to hold the glass chimney, and a shade which may be of silk or glass. The oil container is most often of metal (usually brass), glass or china and is supported in various ways, sometimes on a pedestal moulded as part of the container, sometimes on a long stem, sometimes in a ring which is either supported by a bracket or hung by chains from the ceilings. There is also a type which is carried by a handle attached to the container.

If lamps are in a fixed position on stage they can work off the mains; if they are moved or carried they must be battery-operated.

If the lamp is to be made the container and base can be modelled, moulded and cast, preferably in fibreglass, or they can be turned in wood, or some suitably shaped urn or vase can be adapted. If it is to be battery-operated enough space must be left in the base to accommodate the battery and there should be a removable plate or section to allow for changing it. A switch, of the toggle or button type, should also be incorporated into the base. Another point to remember is that it must be possible to carry a wire to the bulb without its being exposed. A real lamp fitting should be bought, as it is really very difficult to make the collar, wick winders and gallery. This mechanism will have a fitting at the bottom to go over or into the neck of the container and it must be adapted by the electrician to carry a light bulb. Shaped glass chimneys can also be bought, but they are fragile, so it is safer to use a plexiglas tube, or a roll of clear acetate, or thin plastic sheeting (of the kind used to insulate windows). The size of the tube will depend on that of the gallery. If this means that the tube is too small to go over the lamp bulb, vertical cuts can be made in the tube to accommodate the bulb.

The finished lamp can, of course, be painted or foiled and decorated to suit the production and a shade can be bought or made. The glass globe type may be made from a plastic lamp shade, obtainable from most department stores, and a cut glass or engraved effect produced by incising a design into the surface with a small soldering iron, accentuating it with white paint rubbed into the surface. Silk shades for oil lamps were often very elaborate and, given time, are enjoyable to make. Buy or make a wire frame (it is usual to use copper wire) of the shape you need and cover it with Jap silk of whatever colour you choose. Sew the silk on round the widest part of the frame, and gather it in for the smallest part, stretching it firmly between the two. It can then be spread again if there is another wide ring. Trim the shade with braid, lace, fringe, or gathered frills of the silk. Ribbons, bows or even artificial flowers or feathers can be used for decoration. A shade holder, which will rest on the gallery, can be bought from lighting shops or department stores. The lamp bulb itself will have to be lacquered with amber or yellow to give the right coloured light for oil.

Gas

Gasoliers and wall brackets can be hired or bought. Remember that the gas passes to the burner through a pipe or tube which has a tap attachment to cut off the flow. As gas rises, the burner is set pointing upwards and there is nearly always a mantle which intensifies the light. This is usually covered by a shade, but because the mantle is quite large, it makes the use of a normal sized light bulb convincing. Sometimes gas fittings have a pilot jet, and the gas is ignited or extinguished by pulling one of two short chains attached to a pivoted arm situated on the pipe just below the burner.

If the shade is to be a glass globe it can be made as described for oil lamps; if it is to be tulip shaped, it can be cast in fibreglass. If you are hiring the fittings you will almost certainly find that the hire firms carry shades and provide them with the fittings.

Electricity

Hire firms should be able to supply virtually anything you need in the way of electric fittings: period feeling can be achieved with the type of shade used.

Candles

The candle shown in fig. 18 is made from cardboard tube coated with a layer of glass fibre mat and resin. The wax drips are made from resin paste, which was allowed to run and form pools over the base. The light fitting is again a metal tube with a small lamp concealed inside it. There is a 2 in. (5 cm.) long section of clear cinemoid (used in stage lamps) glued to the top of the tube, to give the illusion of transparent wax. The tops are cut unevenly as large candles of this type never seem to burn evenly. Period wax candles were not white paraffin wax, so breaking down, normally to a beeswax colour, is essential.

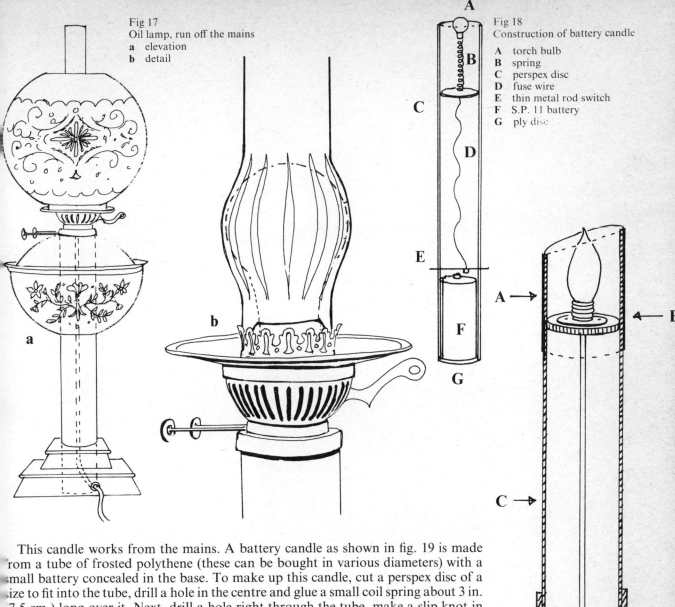

Fig 17
Oil lamp, run off the mains
a elevation
b detail

Fig 18
Construction of battery candle

A torch bulb
B spring
C perspex disc
D fuse wire
E thin metal rod switch
F S.P. 11 battery
G ply disc

This candle works from the mains. A battery candle as shown in fig. 19 is made from a tube of frosted polythene (these can be bought in various diameters) with a small battery concealed in the base. To make up this candle, cut a perspex disc of a size to fit into the tube, drill a hole in the centre and glue a small coil spring about 3 in. (7·5 cm.) long over it. Next, drill a hole right through the tube, make a slip knot in some fuse wire, leaving a loop, solder a small metal plate on to the loop near the knot and drop it down inside the tube. Pass a small metal rod about the size of a darning needle into the hole, through the loop on the wire and out at the other hole in the tube. Pull the knot tight, thus forming a switch. The other end of the wire can now be fed through the hole in the disc and the spring and wired to a small bulb holder which must then be fixed to the top of the spring. Now glue the disc inside the tube, and insert a very small flame-shaped bulb. Push the battery into the other end of the tube so that the contact is very near the fabricated switch, and cork it in with a cork or plywood disc. When the lighted candle is carried the spring moves, giving precisely the effect of a flickering candle.

Log fires

To give the appearance of half-burned logs, cut two short sections of cardboard tube, the diameter of the log required. Space the two pieces to the length of log needed with a piece of galvanized wire, and tape the wire to the tube. Wrap white millinery

Fig 19
Construction of candle run off the mains

A cinemoid
B ply disc
C cardboard tube
D holder

buckram, which has been soaked in warm water, lengthways along this structure and wire it to make one tube. The middle will be transparent, and appear to be burning, when lit from underneath. Block the open ends of the tube with large corks or wooden discs. Make several logs for one fire and wire them firmly together. Paint the ends a dark blackish-brown, or cover them with brown velvet, broken down. Leave the middle section bare. When the logs are lit from underneath with a red lamp, the effect is surprisingly realistic. A small flicker wheel, of the type used in coal-effect electric fires, could also be incorporated, but this will only be really effective on a small stage, or when the stage is dimly lit, or perhaps in a fireplace that is on stage for the entire play. A further step towards realism is to incorporate a small electric fan (pointing upwards) at the back of the fire and tie a few strips of flame-coloured silk to a wire immediately above the fan blades. By carefully angling the lamp, it is possible to catch the moving silk occasionally in the light, producing an effect that may deceive even the fireman.

27 The candles from the London Coliseum production of *Il Trovatore*, 1973. Photo: Anthony Crickmay

Coal fires

The electrical department will supply a board to fit the fireplace, mounted with the lamps which are to be used for the fire light. Make a mound of wire mesh to fit over

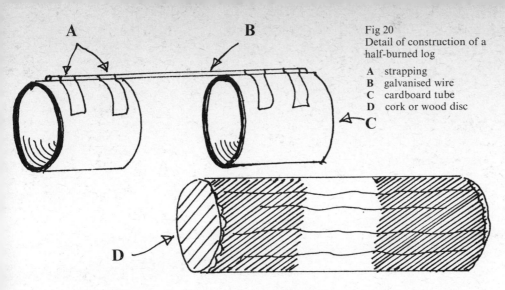

Fig 20
Detail of construction of a half-burned log

A strapping
B galvanised wire
C cardboard tube
D cork or wood disc

them and cover it with fibreglass resin and matting. If orange pigment is added to the resin it will obviate colouring the light with cinemoid; some red F.E.V. can be dabbed on to the fibreglass when it is dry to give variety of colour. Then make some lumps of coal from polystyrene, scrim them, then paint them black on the top, red underneath, and glue them to the mound. Light up the fire and add more paint or coal until the effect is realistic.

Special and Trick Props

ROGER OLDHAMSTEAD

It is part of the theatrical illusion that certain things, which cannot possibly happen, appear to happen night after night on the stage. These will almost certainly call for special props, sometimes of a purely mechanical nature, the making of which demands ingenuity and imagination and may involve various skills and knowledge beyond those generally used in prop making.

No matter what the prop maker is called on to produce, he should keep it as simple as possible; clever mechanical contrivances can, and often do, go wrong at embarrassing moments. One piece of string is worth a stage full of sophisticated machinery and if it does fail, it is easy to put right.

Dummies

As dead bodies seem to appear fairly regularly on stage, some advice on their construction is relevant here. Accuracy is important and the prop maker should first study a reference book on anatomy to learn how a skeleton is constructed and how the bones and muscles work together.

An articulated wood or metal skeleton built to correct human proportions is a basic necessity. The shoulders and hips should move in the appropriate directions and the elbows, knees, wrists, and ankles given their limited movement (which will become obvious if the prop maker studies his own or someone else's joints). This skeleton can be covered or bound with several different materials, from old soft rags, through cotton waste wadding, to the expensive but perfect corpse-making material, Dacron wadding. (This is normally used in upholstery, but is now increasingly used as a replacement for heavy padding in Falstaffian figures, and as an interfacing in period clothes generally, since it is very light and virtually uncrushable.) When the figure has been padded out to shape, it should be bound smoothly in strips of scrim, butter muslin, or any soft, slightly stretchy fabric. If the figure is to be handled or carried, weight, in the form of sandbags or lead shot, will have to be incorporated in the layers of padding on all the limbs, the back, shoulders, head and hips. If sand is used, fill plastic bags and seal them well before covering them in tightly woven canvas or burlap. Sand has a habit of getting out of any container, and while a trail of blood across the stage would be highly impressive, a trail of sand would not.

Head and hands

Unless the prop maker is a trained sculptor or has the patience and ability to model head and hands, life casts should be used (see chapter on Moulding and Casting). The moulds will have to be made in two pieces. After the life mask has been taken, a

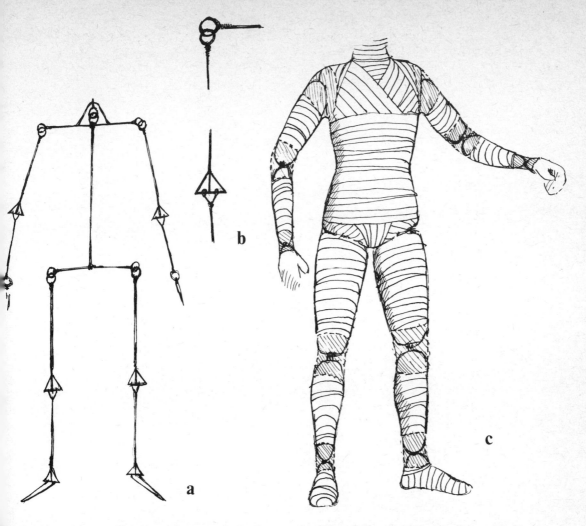

positive in plaster will have to be cast, from the mould. The neck and the back of the head will then have to be built up on to it with clay and a fresh mould made. To do this build a clay wall round the head and neck, dividing the back from the front. Grease the face of the cast and the clay wall with soap or petroleum jelly and make the mould of this half. When the plaster is set, remove the clay wall and grease the plaster so revealed. Grease the back of the head and mould it. When it is set the two parts of the mould can be strapped together for casting the head. To make a mould of a hand, press the well greased hand, palm downwards, into a bed of clay, which must be greased, and then pour the plaster over the back of the hand. When it is set, lift the hand and the plaster and turn it over. Grease the revealed plaster, and mould the palm side of the hand. This will produce a two-piece mould which can be cast in the same way as the head. Casts taken with latex rubber and casting foam (diphynl methane) give the most lifelike effect. Casting foam is a liquid form of sponge plastic composed of two chemicals mixed in equal quantities with an electric beater or drill attachment. Latex is painted into the mould and allowed to dry. This process is repeated two or three times to build up a good layer. The mould is then filled with casting foam which will expand to fill it. A cover should be placed over the openings of the moulds while the foam is expanding. As the foam sticks to most surfaces on setting (from mixing to setting takes less than three minutes, so it is advisable to have all tools, and moulds, as well as some assistance, to hand), the latex surface will adhere to the foam and not to the mould surface. The result will be a soft, flexible cast, with a realistic 'skin'.

Fig 21
Construction of a dummy

a   skeleton
b   joints
c   padding and binding

Great care should be taken when handling the foam; rubber gloves should be worn
at all times, and the work carried out in a well ventilated room, avoiding direct
inhalation of any gases given off. The exact quantity of foam required depends, of
course, on the size of the mould, but it is useful to remember that the foam expands
to at least ten times its own liquid volume.

The casts can then be fixed to the armature, the hands can be drilled out and the
ends of the arms of the skeleton, inserted and glued in; the head can be glued to the
neck of the armature in the same way. The figure can then be given the additional
refinements of false eyelashes and glass eyes, if they are available. These are inserted
simply by making a slit in the head and pushing them in, with a little glue or cement
to hold them.

If latex rubber and foam are not available, quite an acceptable head can be modelled
up and cast from a plaster mould in polyester resin or papier-mâché (see chapter on
Moulding and Casting). As dummy corpses are normally used in highly dramatic
situations, full attention to realism and painstaking finishing are essential. Smooth
skin texture, a good wig and good make-up can only work provided the basic shape
has been well made. Again, remember that the arm and leg joints in the human body
are limited in movement, elbows and knees only moving one way. Many figures are
spoilt by a failure to observe this basic anatomical fact. Another point worth remem-
bering is that a human head weighs about 10 lbs. (4·5 kg.) and that an adult male can
weigh upwards of 150 lbs. (68 kg.), so a lot of weight will have to be put into handled
figures.

Painting a figure and finishing
Figures can be painted with acrylic paints, obtainable from any art suppliers. These
are preferable to scenic paints because they are translucent and can be applied in thin
washes. The exposed parts of the skin should first be painted a uniform opaque beige

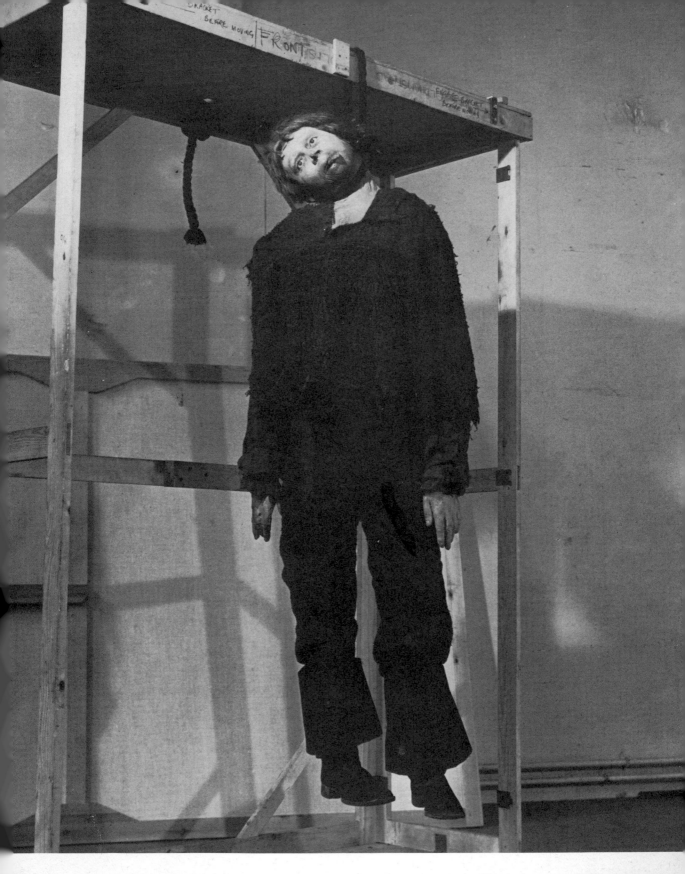

pink, paler than skin tone; this can be done with scenic colour and emulsion medium. When this is dry, an even wash of skin colour acrylic paint should be brushed on and allowed to dry. To get good flesh colour, match it to the colour of your own hand or arm. Under stage lights the colour will usually be found to be too light rather than too dark, so mix a little red with a small quantity of the wash and apply it to the cheeks, chin, forehead, nose, ears, backs of hands, etc. Check your own face in a mirror for lighter and darker patches. If the dummy represents a member of the cast, the face should be made up in the same way as that of the actor in question. It should be remembered, of course, that dead faces are pale. Soft beards and moustaches can be simulated, as can hair on the arms and legs, by painting or spraying the skin with an adhesive and, when it becomes tacky, dragging a small piece of soft fur across it.

The whole figure will normally have to be sprayed down with black or brown paint when finished, as dummies tend to look a little too new or too dominant under stage light. An air brush or mouth spray will give the desired effect. Too much will look dirty, so experiment under light if possible and preferably with someone else there for comparison. Clothing must be sewn in place as it tends to slip with handling.

Dolls can be treated quite differently from dummies, because they are supposed to look artificial. A solid, non-flexible body and limbs can be constructed, without the bother of weight and movement. A doll such as Olympia in Offenbach's *Tales of Hoffman*, which has to be pulled apart on stage, can be made by adapting a display dummy with joints which are designed to come apart easily, being of the peg and socket type.

Props to be broken

Bottles, glasses, mirrors and china are regularly broken for effect. It would be easy to use the real thing, but safety and expense have to be considered. The traditional way of making breakable glass bottles is by casting them in sugar which has been boiled to a hard toffee state and poured into a mould, itself a cast of a bottle. This is a long and trying process, and the same effect can be produced by painting the inside of the mould with a clear non-reinforced polyester resin, letting it set and repeating two or three times until a reasonable thickness is obtained. But the bottles made in this way should not be used for breaking over the head as they are still very hard.

Clear panes of glass can be made with one of the clear plastic embedding resins, poured on to a glass or plastic sheet to which the resin will not adhere.

While on the subject of breaking china and glass, it may be useful to indicate here how to strengthen fragile objects. There are certain occasions when the use of real china or glass cannot be avoided, for example, practical tea services or wine decanters, glasses and vases. To prevent glasses shattering and leaving dangerous splinters, they must be scrimmed (i.e. closely covered) with fine net, using a spray adhesive or P.V.A.-based adhesive. Spraying or painting the scrimmed surface with varnish or shellac both strengthens and makes the fabric translucent. China can be treated in a similar way, but in this case it is better to use butter muslin or silk for the scrimming. It is also possible to enamel over the fabric and paint on designs.

In Chekhov's *Three Sisters* a china clock has to be smashed. This can be done by finding a suitable clock case and making a mould of it, from which the necessary number of casts can be taken. These should be of plaster of paris which has been allowed to dry out very thoroughly as wet plaster is heavy and won't break cleanly. The cast is best made hollow. Pour plaster into the mould and shake it around inside until it coats well, then pour off the surplus. When thoroughly set, the cast will be very thin walled and light. The surface of the plaster can be primed with shellac and painted with enamel in imitation of the model from which the mould was made. The face and works of the clock can be slipped into a new cast every night. The thickness of the cast should be adjusted until the right kind of breaking is produced; if it is too thin the pieces will be too small. Even clay, which has a tendency to be brittle, can be modelled and allowed to dry out; more solid and compact objects are best suited to this treatment, however, because of the crumbly nature of the clay.

30 A realistic head made from latex and foam plastic, used in *The Bassarides*, 1974, and a doll's head with wig from *The Tales of Hoffmann*, 1970, both London Coliseum productions. Photo: Donald Southern

Wax is another material that lends itself to casting and is particularly suitable for bottles and china which have to be broken. It also has the virtue of being able to hold cold liquids. Pour molten wax into the mould, roll it around until it has cooled, and then remove the cast. The disadvantage of wax is that it is so delicate it may break before it is meant to, but it is very satisfactory for objects which have to be thrown at someone on the stage as it is very light and does not have any cutting edges. Wax may be painted or sprayed with emulsion or acrylic paints. Its great advantage is that it can be melted down and reused again and again.

For most objects it will be necessary to make a mould in two pieces. The methods for doing this described in the section on heads and hands need only slight adaptation for such things as bottles.

Breaking weapons

The assorted weaponry that a prop maker is called upon to produce ranges from the relative simplicity of a knife which appears to draw blood, to the very special weapons that are required, for example, for Wagner's *Ring Cycle*.

A hollow-bladed knife with a tube inside it leading to a rubber bulb filled with stage blood concealed in the handle will work very well, and is often used to produce 'cuts' on hands and faces. But a sword that has to break in half, as if by magic, without any contact with any other object, is another matter. The problem was solved in the following way for the English National Opera's production of *The Ring*. Take the blade, cut it into its broken pieces and back the upper half with a further piece of jagged metal. Add a short peg on to the extension piece, drilling a hole in the broken end to match when the pieces are lined up. The piece with the hole becomes the back of the sword. Then fix a strip of metal, with clips, to the back of the sword to cover the hole and extend beyond it for a further 2 or 3 in. (5–7·5 cm.). The broken piece is thus held between the extension and the metal strip and so cannot fall. Attach the strip, which is able to slide in the clips, to a lever in the handle of the sword. When this lever is drawn back, pulling the strip with it, clear of the hole, the broken blade is free to fall. Provided the strip is in position over the hole the sword may be wielded quite happily. The weapon for this production had the added sophistication of a spring release in the handle and was made by a professional metal worker. But, although welding was used here, it is possible to construct a weapon of this kind using rivets and epoxy resin, and sheet aluminium instead of steel.

Blood

Blood has already been mentioned but it deserves a few words of its own here. A successful method of producing a limited amount, perhaps just to smear the face or hands, is to use a ring, in which the original setting has been replaced by a small cube of sponge soaked in stage blood. The ring is worn with the setting facing inwards, and gentle pressure on the sponge produces enough blood to show, as a little goes a long way. There are many proprietary brands of blood available from all theatrical make-up suppliers, and they will wash off. These can be used on dummies, with the addition of a small quantity of emulsion medium. It is also possible to mix paint the appropriate colour, but it should be tested under the lights as stage blood often looks too pink; there should be plenty of depth and body in the colour.

Some examples of trick props

Every situation is different and every designer has his or her own ideas. It is not necessary, as I have said before, to become complicated, nor is a degree in engineering necessary or even desirable. As with all prop making, the finish and assurance with which something is made are worth more than any number of gadgets or radio-controlled motors.

It is only possible to give a few examples here, in the hope that the methods described can be adapted for other problems.

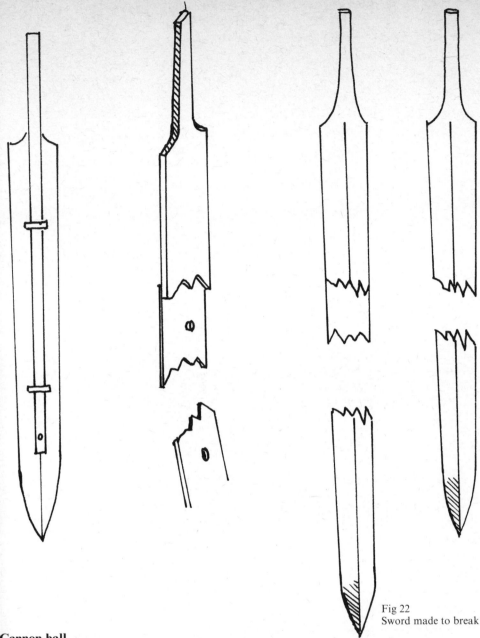

Fig 22
Sword made to break

Cannon ball

In Prokofiev's *War and Peace* a cannon ball is required to land at the feet of Napoleon. He then has to kick it a short distance away from him. As a cannon ball cannot be thrown on stage with any accuracy, it was decided in the English National Opera's production to conceal the ball in the floor, below a pair of small trap doors. As the stage was on a rake, the ball itself had to be weighted to prevent it rolling too far. The diagram illustrates the use of 'one piece of string' referred to earlier, although mechanical means could be used. The ball is propelled upwards in its cradle by means of a rod, and forces open the trap doors. These close behind it, by means of springs, and the ball is left on the stage. The opening of the trap was masked by synchronizing it with a flash from a flash box set 6 in. (15 cm.) down stage of the trap doors. The ball was cast in fibreglass in two sections and lined in $\frac{1}{4}$ in. (0·63 cm.) foam rubber. Then a small quantity of lead shot was added to the inside and the pieces joined. This arrangement allowed the ball to roll when kicked but it stopped almost at once.

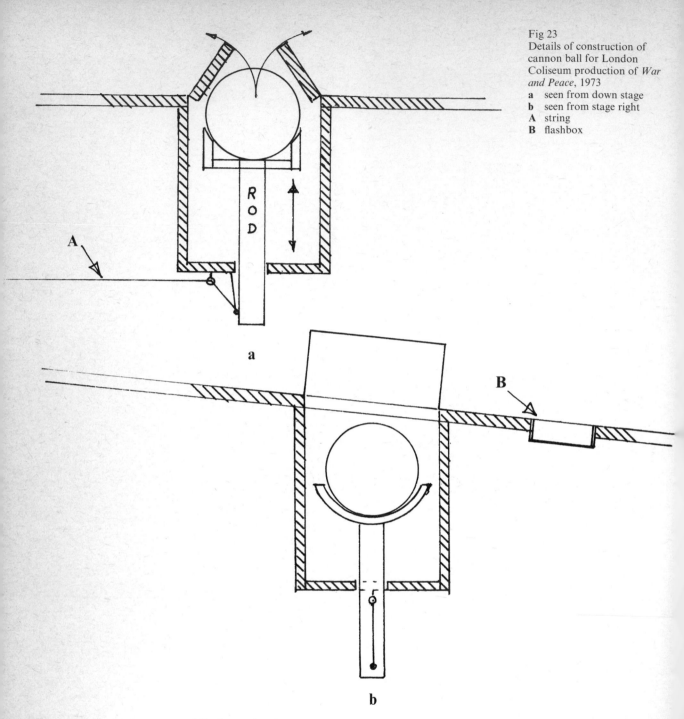

Fig 23
Details of construction of
cannon ball for London
Coliseum production of *War
and Peace*, 1973
a seen from down stage
b seen from stage right
A string
B flashbox

a

b

Moving animals

Small animals can be made to jump or hop by building into them a small air valve
shutter release of the type used on photographic equipment. The valve is inserted into
the body at such an angle as to produce a lift forward, as in the diagram of the toad
About 14 in. (35 cm.) long, the toad is made of polystyrene foam with articulated
wooden limbs. The skin is cotton jersey, painted and textured with latex before being
added to the frame. Small perspex half spheres were used for the eyes. The total weight
is about 2 lbs. (1 kg.) and the largest type of valve was used, giving enough lift to move
the creature forward about 6 in. (15 cm.). The air release is normally supplied with

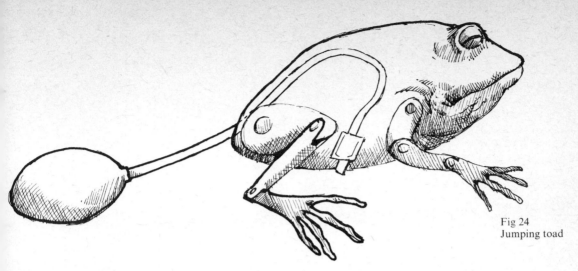

Fig 24
Jumping toad

about 6 ft. (2 m.) of tubing and a rubber bulb with a valve. In this case the toad was placed on a 'rock' at about table height and the tube and bulb dropped down behind to be operated by a member of the cast.

Flying bird

First hire or construct (see chapter on Hand Props) a bird with wings spread. Screw two small pulleys, one at each end of a 3 × 1 in. (7·5 × 2·5 cm.) batten and pass a length of sash cord through them, pulling through about 12 ft. (4 m.) of cord for the on stage end. Tie a piece of nylon line firmly to this on stage end of the cord. Tie the batten to a bar from the flies and take it up to about 20 ft. (7 m.), not losing hold of the nylon line. Cut the nylon to a length of about 15 ft. (5 m.) and tie it to a small ring. Three nylon stays from the wings and tail will be needed to stop the bird from twisting. Tie them to the ring, finding the point of balance. While holding the bird, fly the bar out of sight. The off stage of the sash cord should be long enough to remain on the stage. Now carry the bird to the point from which the flight is to start, either the fly floor or the top of a tall ladder. Pull the loose ends of the sash cord D to take up the slack. The angle of flight will be governed by the relative positions of the pulley at A and the starting point C. The speed of flight is regulated by the weight of the bird (the lighter the slower). When the bird is released it will fly in a perfect arc from the pulley A; to adjust this and make the bird fly from high to low, pay out the rope D. Various forms of flight can be simulated by pulling in and paying out this cord, but it will need a good deal of rehearsing. The sash cord must be tied off to a cleat at the greatest length and the cord C must be marked at other salient points by wrapping a piece of coloured sellotape (plastic tape) round it. Someone reliable must be stationed to catch the bird at the end of its flight, which must, of course, be out of sight. Nothing gets a bigger laugh than a bird coming back on stage after its exit, backwards.

71

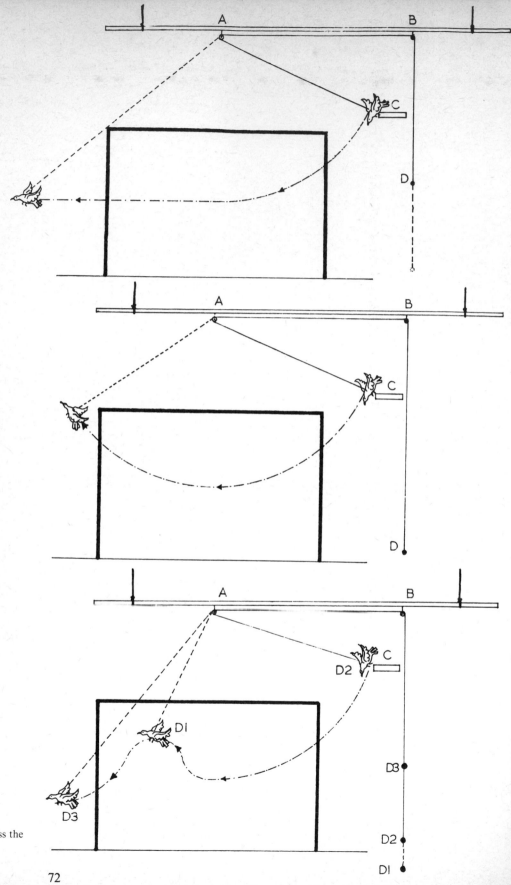

Fig 25
Method of flying bird across the
stage

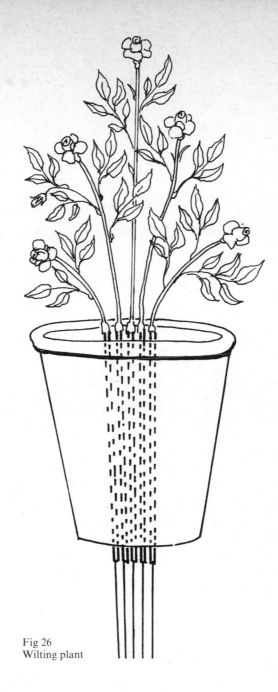

Fig 26
Wilting plant

A wilting plant
Make a form of polystyrene to fit into a flower pot or vase from which the base has
been removed. Set into it three or four $\frac{3}{16}$ in. (0·45 cm.) metal tubes, extending 2 or 3
in. (5 or 7·5 cm.) at top and bottom. Fit over the tops 1 ft. (30 cm.) or more of green
$\frac{3}{16}$ in. (0·45 cm.) rubber tubing. Then cut lengths of steel wire about 6 in. (15 cm.) longer
than the tubes, top them with a metal or plastic cap or a small bead and push them
through the tubes from the bottom; the wires will work effectively even if they are
slightly curved. Cut a hole in the table or shelf on which the plant is to stand and glue
or wire the flower pot over it. The rubber tubing can now be dressed with flowers and
leaves. Someone will have to be posted under the table or shelf to manipulate the
wires; withdrawing them from the tubes will cause the plant to wilt and the reverse can
be effected by pushing them up again.

73

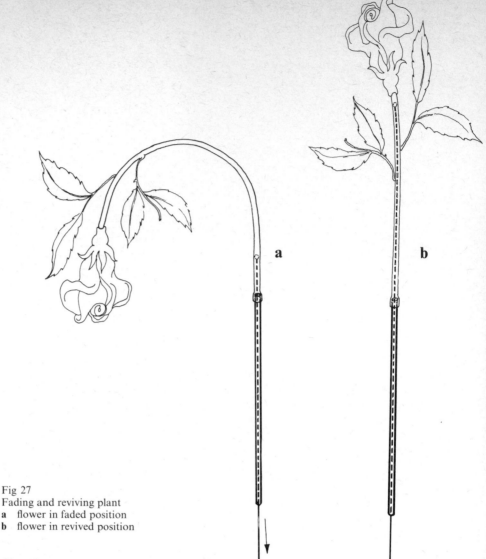

Fig 27
Fading and reviving plant
a flower in faded position
b flower in revived position

Shooting

Shots may be fired on stage at particular objects and bullet holes must appear in the appropriate place. When selecting a target, remember that bullet holes show up better in a light surface. When the place has been chosen, back the area with ply, glued on, and drill bullet holes of a size suitable for the weapon. Hinge another piece of ply to one side of this backing and paint the inside of it black. If the holes are big they can be plugged with corks, which must be painted so that they are camouflaged. With strong glue attach some string to the back of the corks and, as the shot is fired, pull them out sharply and flap the black ply round to cover the holes. If the holes are small, another piece of ply, painted to match the visible surface, can be hinged to the other side of the backing ply and flapped round to cover the holes. As the shot is fired, exchange the two backings by flapping them round. If this is well done it will be convincing; synchronization with the shot is, of course, essential.

If an object has to be hit, tie a nylon thread to it and pass it through the scenery or furniture; by pulling this the object can be made to fall. Something which has to shatter is much more difficult, and the problem varies with the circumstances and the type of object involved; it will certainly have to be pre-broken and put together with spots of a weak adhesive. It can then be pulled with a nylon thread so that it breaks on falling. If the object is hollow, a hole can be drilled under it through the surface on which it stands (and to which it must be fixed), and a rod can be pushed up through the hole to shatter it. This rod can be made to represent part of its armature or construction.

For arrows or thrown knives the traditional method works well. The knife or arrow is hinged to a small plate, with a spring attached to the underside and a stop to the top side. This plate is glued or sewn to the target, which may well be human, and the arrow or knife is then pulled down against the spring and held flat against the surface or body with a breakable cotton thread or a small strap held with a snap fastener (press stud). When this is released the arrow or knife springs up to a horizontal position and quivers most convincingly. Care must be taken, of course, to camouflage the weapon before it is sprung.

A magic gate
A straight run of picket fence with a gate in the middle leaves very little concealment for tricks, but the gate, as in *The Rake's Progress*, may have to open on command and then shut again. To effect this, strap to the bottom of one of the sticks which form the gate, about 6 in. (15 cm.) from the hinge, a piece of metal tubing, which has been drilled at each end with a small hole. It should extend about 3 in. (7·5 cm.) on each side of the gate. Tie a length of nylon fishing line through each of the holes, and carry the lines off stage along each side of the fence. When the ends are out of sight, cut them off and fix toggles. Clearly one line pulls to open and the other to shut the gate.

Falling snow
The usual method of producing a fall of snow is to hang a cloth (an old backcloth will do) from the flies, find the centre between the top and bottom and draw a line across it. Then make a number of vertical slits, each extending 3 or 4 ft. (about 1 m.) each side of the centre line, to cover almost the whole width of the cloth. Then take up the bottom of the cloth on an adjacent set of lines, making a loop of it. Empty a sack of torn up white paper or of chips of polystyrene into the loop of cloth and spread it evenly across the width. Take both lines up so that the cloth is out of sight, and when the time comes for the snow to fall, lift and drop first one set of lines and then the other. The snow paper or chips will fall very realistically.

It must be remembered, when making any kind of trick prop or special effect, that finish and not the final mechanics involved are of prime importance. A technically well made prop that has a poor finish due to the amount of time spent on its working parts will only be a disappointment, both artistically for the maker and visually for the audience. A special effect is usually required to make a dramatic point at a crucial moment in a play or opera, especially in the latter, where violence and tragedy abound. It can rapidly degenerate into comedy if, for example, heads that bounce if dropped are allowed on stage.

Masks and animal heads
The tradition and use of masks is very ancient and is a huge subject, needing a whole book to itself if it is to be discussed in detail, but the technique for making them is generally the same as for the other moulds and casts discussed here, except for a few methods of using fabrics to make them light and comfortable to wear and act in.

There are as many possibilities for mask design as there are for costume and as there are types of plays. They can be full masks, half masks, comic or tragic masks, carnival masks or false noses, they can be used for suggesting age, the supernatural or fantastic, or for disguises. Heads can be for grotesque figures, real, fantastic or pantomimic animals. They can suggest animals, perhaps by ears and some fur, or by purely decorative fabrics and design, or they can be an attempt to get as near to the real proportions and details as possible, with a full head.

The masks discussed and illustrated here are both from *A Midsummer Night's Dream*. The ass's head made no attempt at realism, but was a light suggestion very

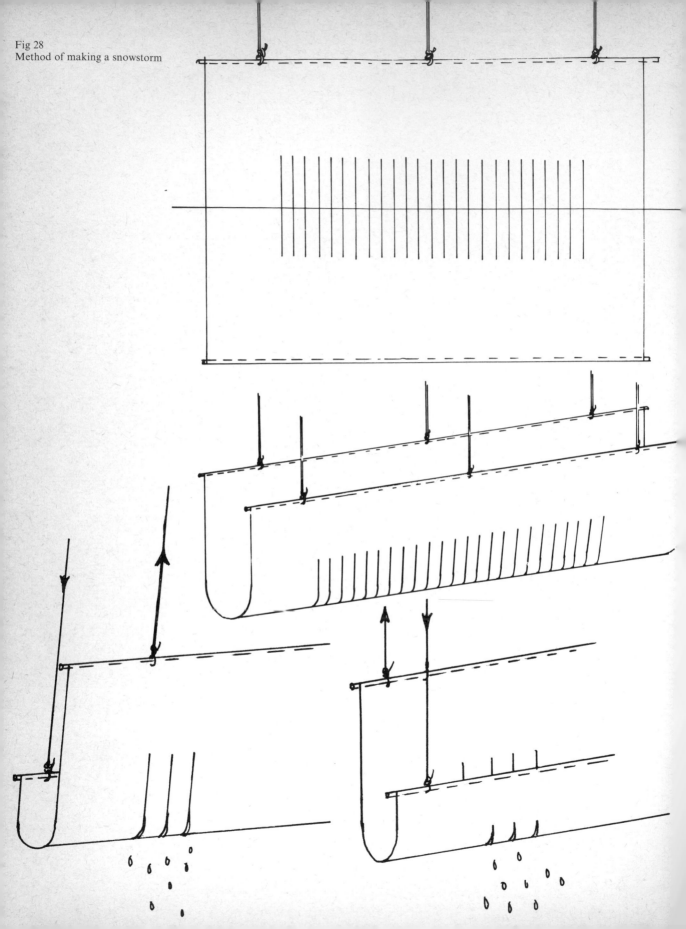

Fig 28
Method of making a snowstorm

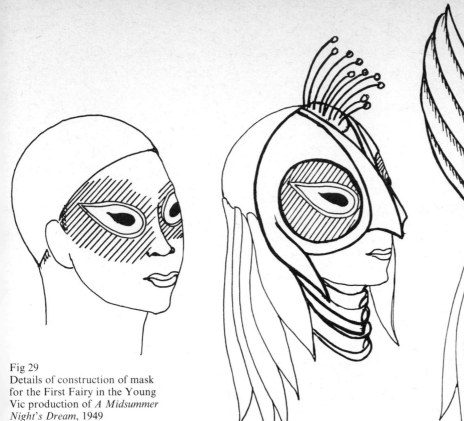

Fig 29
Details of construction of mask
for the First Fairy in the Young
Vic production of *A Midsummer
Night's Dream*, 1949

easy for the actor to manipulate. The mask for the first fairy was again very light and
was part of the headdress.

A life cast was made of the actress's face and on this the mask was modelled, making
it as delicate and unenveloping as possible. A mould was made from this, in which the
mask was cast in chamois leather, painted in with shellac. When it was set and taken
out the edge was wired with hat wire and bound with more leather. It then received
several more coats of shellac before it was painted with emulsion.

A very close fitting jersey cap was made for the actress in which she could hide her
hair, and the mask was sewn to it. The hair, also sewn on, was made of feathers cut
from vilene and painted, and springy wire with small beads on the ends were threaded
through the forehead of the mask to make the comb. The wing pieces were cut from
buckram, wired round the edges and more vilene feathers were applied and scrimmed
and painted over where they were joined to the mask, making them seem to be all one
piece. A thin jersey fabric was draped across the front of the neck, up to the cap, and
this was also painted and sprayed.

The ass's head had a close fitting calico cap fastened under the chin, and a foam
rubber roll covered with jersey fabric was sewn to the cap. The lower jaw, which was
articulated by the actor's own jaw, had a light cane frame. The cane is somewhat
unpredictable so the actual construction has to be worked out as it is formed and
loops of cane added where it needs support and shaping.

It was lined with pink calico and white felt teeth were added round the inner rim of
the jaw. A cup was made to fit over the chin and the jaw was sewn to this, and two
elastic straps were fixed to the mask, one to fasten round the back of the neck and the
other to come from the jaw to the temple (this helps the jaw to close). Then the outside
was covered with thin pale grey felt and sprayed and painted.

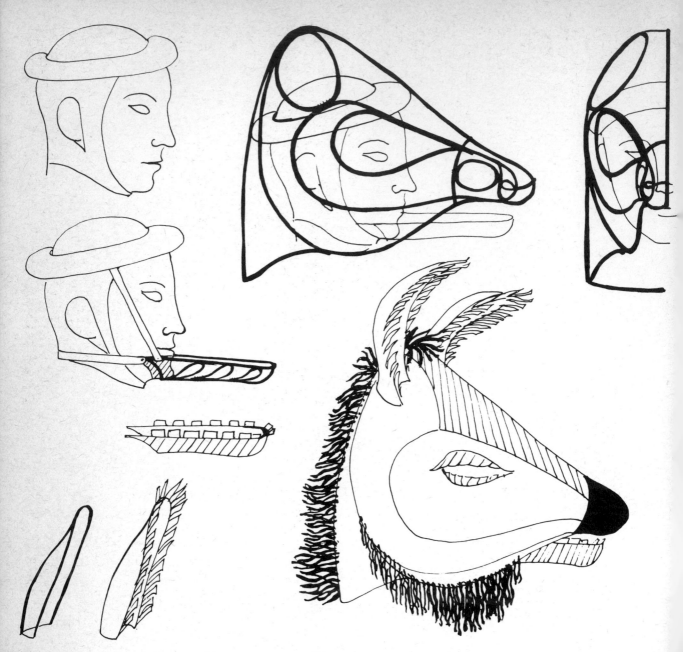

Fig 30
Construction of ass's
head

Next the head was made, fine cane again forming the main shape with as few joins in the cane as possible. Where joins were unavoidable the cane ends were bound together with raffia, binding in loops and stays of cane where necessary. The whole head was covered with stiff grey muslin or tarlatan, then grey felt was applied (indicated by shading in the diagram). The eye was made of black felt and the eyelashes of fringed white felt and these were stuck on. The ear shapes were made from a thinner cane, so that they would be floppy, and lined with thin pink calico with a white felt fringe round the edges. The back was covered with thin grey felt. They were then sewn into place supported by part of the frame. The mane and beard was made of black raffia, or it could be wool. The head was jammed down on to the padded roll and had an extra elastic strap under the chin for safety. It needed many fittings and adjustments before it was absolutely right and comfortable, but it was finally very light and easy and the actor could see and breathe without any trouble.

Carpentry Props

HAYDEN GRIFFIN

Introduction

Apart from its use in the general structure of scenery, wood may be required for the construction of a wide variety of props. Interior sets need furniture, doors and windows (and, occasionally, the mouldings that go around them), exterior sets may need trees, fences, gates or benches.

While many items may, of course, be hired, the cost of this for the run of a show can be very high, and therefore, if time allows, it is more sensible to make the relatively simple pieces. This, usually, works out cheaper and they can be stored for use in other shows. There may in fact be no alternative to designing and making something to fit a specific piece of direction in a show, or to fit the setting. Again, it may be difficult to find something the right size, weight, and manoeuvrability for the stage.

Because the possible variations of use and style are enormous, I will discuss in detail only a few selected items in the hope that this will lead to a broader and more general view of how wood can be employed as a material in the construction of stage properties. The items I have described have been chosen either because they incorporate constructional methods which are applicable to many different articles which may be needed in a show and which may be difficult to find, or because the real thing would be too difficult to manage on stage. As this is not intended as a carpentry manual but a basic guide, I will not go into too much technical detail about the construction. With a bit of imagination, any of the methods may be adapted for other items which may be needed.

1 Exterior furniture and weathering wood   Example: a bench

Benches are a very useful seating device on stage: the one described here is an outdoor bench, slightly ageing and weather-worn. It is 6 ft. (2 m.) long, with a back, and while it looks 'period' and 'rural', it is not tied to a specific time or place.

Pine deal, the cheapest suitable wood, is very easily obtainable. Because of its softness it is ideal for ageing easily and distinctively. A bench of this length should be strong enough to seat three or even four people, if necessary, and for this the timber of the seat planks should be at least $1\frac{1}{4}$ to $1\frac{1}{2}$ in. (3 to 4 cm.) thick. Old scaffold boards are ideal but if they are unobtainable, $9 \times 1\frac{1}{2}$ in. ($22 \cdot 5 \times 4$ cm.) unfinished deal is stocked by most timber yards. The frame is of 2 in. (5 cm.) square pine deal mortised and tenoned together in the shape of an angular 'h', the long stroke being the back-rest support and leg and the rest representing the flat base of the seat and the front leg. Half-lap joints can be used but they should be strengthened by pegging with dowel pins. The back 2 in. (5 cm.) square pillar is 36 in. (92 cm.) high to carry the back rest

Fig 31
A 'rural' bench

which is made up of another $9 \times 1\frac{1}{2}$ in. (22.5×4 cm.) plank.

Assembly: after the frames have been made another bar, parallel to the horizontal of the 'h' should be attached, about $1\frac{1}{2}$ to 2 in. (4 to 5 cm.) above the bottom of the legs. This is also mortised and tenoned in position. Cut a piece of 2×1 in. (5×2.5 cm.) timber 5 ft. 6 in. (1·68 m.) long and mortise and tenon each end to the centre of the lower bar of the framework. This strengthened bar is supplemented by the fixing of the seating and back rest planks to make the whole structure stable.

The depth of the seat should be 18 in. (45 cm.) to be comfortable. This is the width of the two 9 in. (22·5 cm.) boards together. The upper bar of the frame should be 14 in. (35 cm.) long with the front leg jointed into it from below to give maximum strength. The average seat height is 18 in. (45 cm.), so, taking into account the thickness of the seating planks, the front legs should be $14\frac{1}{2}$ in. (36·25 cm.) high with the width of the upper bar supplying the remaining 2 in. (2·5 cm.) of the height. This bar should be jointed into the back pillar $14\frac{1}{2}$ in. (36·25 cm.) from the bottom, thus forming the square 'h'. The bottom cross bar will therefore measure 12 in. (30 cm.) when jointed into the legs.

Taking a measurement from centre to centre of the two frames (spaced by the centre tie between them), measure this out on to the three 9 in. (22·5 cm.) planks and mark this point with a line across the planks. Now align one of the planks on the seat support bars against the back supports. Mark off the position of these bars on to the plank and cut through these marks to the depth of 1 in. (2·5 cm.). Cut this 1 in. (2·5 cm.) section out. The plank can now be notched into the back supports. When the second seat plank is laid in position it will project 1 in. (2·5 cm.) at the front. Now drill two $\frac{1}{4}$ in. (0·63 cm.) holes, evenly spaced, through each of the marked centre lines of the planks and into the support bars. After filling the holes with wood glue, insert $\frac{1}{4}$ in. (0·63 cm.) dowel pegs into the holes and push firmly home. Fix the back rest plank in the same way. When the glue has dried, cut the dowel flush with the planks.

The bench should now be a firm, solid construction. To finish it and to give the appearance of age and weathering, first round off all sharp edges on the frames and planks with a chisel and surform. Now, using a blow lamp (blow torch) burn all the surfaces of the bench, varying the degree of charring here and there. Burn the edges especially. When this is done, use a very hard wire brush to brush off all the charred wood; this will give a weathered appearance since the softer parts of the grain will have burned far more than the hard parts, giving a very strong pattern of the wood grain. When all the charred wood has been removed, the wood should be painted with a very thin transparent mix of grey paint. Finally burnish the bench where it would be worn by people sitting on it. This polishes the hard grain and completes the weathered look. The pegs, being of a harder wood, will be slightly higher in profile than the surrounding wood which is what happens naturally when wood wears and weathers.

2 Upholstered and carved furniture   Example: a nineteenth-century sofa

The sofa illustrated is based on a late nineteenth-century example in the art nouveau style.

It is built mainly of plywood. The side pieces are drawn on to $\frac{1}{2}$ in. or $\frac{1}{4}$ in. (1·25 cm. or 0·63 cm.) plywood and fretworked out. The shape should be drawn out when the leg height has been calculated, taking into account the depth of the upholstery on the

Fig 32
Working drawings for
nineteenth-century sofa
a   side elevation
b   front elevation
c   seat section

A $\frac{1}{4}''$ ply with incised flower
    design
B $1\frac{1}{4}''$ deal carved
C $1\frac{1}{4}''$ deal
D $\frac{1}{4}''$ ply
E   back leg
F   upholstered seat

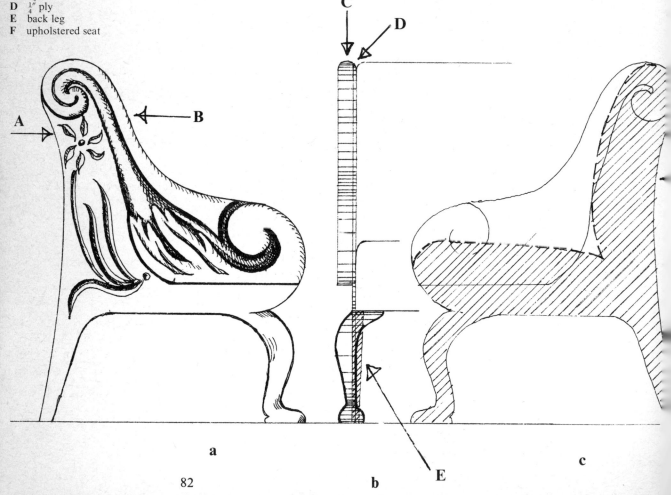

a

b

c

82

seat. The seat and back rest are $\frac{3}{4}$ in. (1·88 cm.) ply and the sides are nailed and glued to them. The decoration on the sides is carved from $1\frac{1}{4}$ in. (1·88 cm.) thick planks profiled to shape and glued to the $\frac{1}{2}$ in. (1·25 cm.) ply profiles. The legs are strengthened and finished by gluing on pre-formed pieces, also carved from deal.

The simplest way to upholster the frame is to cover the back and seat with 3 in. (7·5 cm.) or 4 in. (10 cm.) thick plastic foam, rounding it off at the top of the back and the front edge of the seat. This is then covered with calico (held by tacks to the underside of the plywood seat), which is stretched and fixed well down into the crevice between the back and the seat. When this is firmly tacked down, the calico should be drawn tightly up over the back and tacked to the underneath of the seat. This will pull the plastic foam into a firm, even shape. The chosen upholstery material can then be fixed in the same way. The wooden sides should be stained with a proprietary wood stain and then polished or varnished.

3 Folding and turned furniture   Example: a seventeenth-century folding chair

A piece of furniture seen in a museum or in a painting may seem ideal for a particular production and there should be no great difficulty in copying from either source, though it is obviously preferable to copy from 'life'.

The chair illustrated here was made for the Northcott Theatre, Exeter, production of *Galileo*, and was copied from a chair in an early seventeenth-century etching. It seemed an ideal chair for the main character as it was in period and was also easily portable, which was necessary in the context of the opera. It is based on the folding principle of an x. Each stroke of the x represents an open frame (in this case with carved feet) which articulates on a central spindle either opening to an x or closing almost flat.

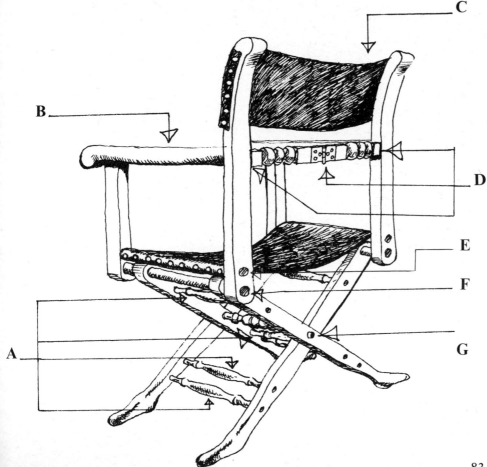

Fig 33
'Period'-type folding chair, adapted from seventeenth-century example

A   formers
B   armrest
C   leather back
D   hinges enabling bar to collapse forwards
E   leather seat support bar
F   leg spindle
G   centre spindle

83

When the leg measurements are being calculated, they should be in proportion to the height of the leather top, fully stretched, at about 18 in. (45 cm.) off the ground. Holes are drilled into the top of the leg frames to allow the lower bar of the arm frame to pass through, but enough leeway should be allowed so that they can move on the spindle, which is the function of this lower bar. The leg frames are completed with cross pieces which can either be of plain dowel or more ornate and turned, as shown in the drawing. The centre spindle should be drilled right through so that a thin metal rod (threaded on both ends) can be inserted on which the frames can articulate. The arm frame is completed with the back support piece, an upright in front and the arm rest. In the drawing the shape has been simplified: obviously if a lathe is available, the back support and the front upright can be made of turned pieces. The final element in the construction of the frame is the seat support bar which is just above the leg spindle, allowing enough room for the leg frames to articulate underneath it.

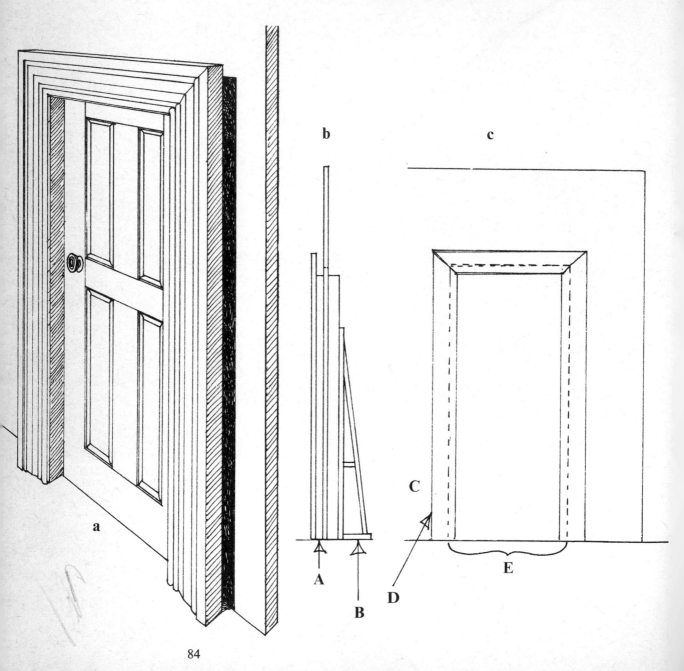

84

The leather seat is attached with brass-headed tacks to the seat support bar. The chair has a leather back attached to the top section of the back supports in the same way. The sides are kept apart by a collapsible stretcher between the two back supports. The bar (simple, or turned as in the drawing) is sawn in half, then the two halves joined by a hinge. Each end of the bar is then attached to the back support with a hinge which moves in the opposite direction to the centre hinge. It will now stay rigid when the two sides are apart but will collapse when pushed forwards in the centre, thus allowing the chair to fold.

Method of assembly: first, construct both leg frame units interlocking them one behind the other before putting in the top 'former' bar. Then insert the centre spindle and push the metal bar through holes drilled at the intersection of both legs and the hole through the centre spindle. Now drill the holes to take the leg spindle on the arm frames. The arm frame should now be attached, having been constructed without the lower bar or leg spindle fixed. The leg spindle should be withdrawn and then threaded back through the arm frame and holes at the top of the legs. The bar can now be glued to the arm frames. It should not be glued to the legs, which should remain freely moving on the bar.

The seat leather should now be attached to the seat support bars as previously described. Next the collapsible 'stretcher' should be attached and, last of all, the leather back rest.

The leather used should be a thick hide to give the best results, and the framework must be strong, hard wood. Pine is too weak at the intersection points. The chair can now be finished by staining the wood to the right colour and polishing either with wax or with french polish. The leather can be 'antiqued' by darkening around the areas which would not be worn and lightening and polishing the areas which would be. If it is built with a reasonable amount of care it should be indistinguishable from the original.

4 Mouldings

Most period interiors to the 1930s have moulding on the framework around doors or windows. When constructing these for the stage it is quite easy (and cheaper than having mouldings specially milled) to build up a pattern which looks authentic with a selection of the numerous simple milled pieces kept by most timber merchants or handicraft shops. These can be supplemented with $\frac{1}{2}$ in. (1·25 cm.) dowel and square sections to build up as ornate a moulding as necessary. They can be tacked and glued to the frame, which should be part of the door structure, and then painted.

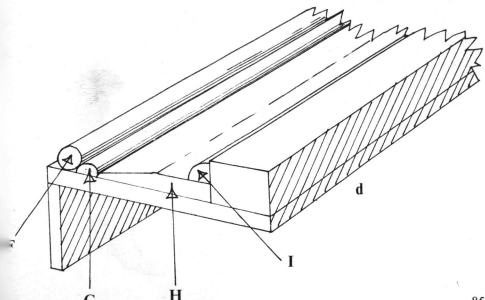

Fig 34
Door moulding and method of preventing flat from moving when door slams
a   door braced just in front of flat
b   side elevation of door frame and flat
c   front elevation of door frame and flat
d   moulding details

A   gap between door and flat
B   door separately braced from flat
C   flat
D   door frame
E   opening in flat allowing clearance around door frame
F   dowel
G $\frac{1}{2}$ round
H   picture rail
I $\frac{1}{4}$ round

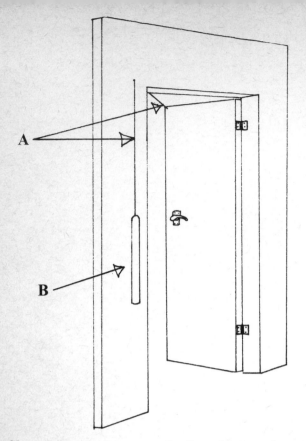
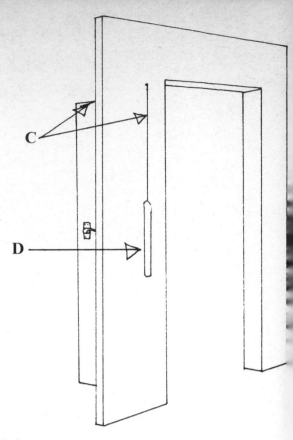

Fig 35
Methods of keeping doors open,
or making sure they shut

A & C nylon line
B & D weights

5 Some hints on doors and sash windows

Most of the infuriating things that happen during the technical part of a stage production are to do with doors. They either don't shut when they should or perversely refuse
to remain open when it is most important that they do so!

The simple way of keeping a door open or making sure it shuts is to counterweight
it behind the flat. This can be done by attaching a bag filled with sand, bolts, or lead
shot with a nylon thread to the top of the door. This thread is led through a tiny hole
in the framework of the flat allowing the weight to hang out of sight behind the flat.
This weight is rigged behind the hinge or on the opposite side of the door depending
on whether it needs to be kept shut or held open. The weight in the bag can be adjusted
so the door can be shut slowly and quietly after an entrance.

Another thing which often happens is that a supposedly solid wall shakes (wobbling
pictures and any other hanging dressing) when the door is slammed by an actor making a dramatic exit or entrance. It is quite unreasonable to ask the actor to 'be careful'
and it is, anyway, obviously useful to be able to slam a door on a set. Quite apart from
being a useful technical device for emphasising a line or situation it helps to achieve
a feeling of naturalness on a set if it can be used as a real room would be.

The problem can be overcome simply by making the door and its frame as separate
constructions, leaving a space in the flat some 2 or 3 in. (5 or 7·5 cm.) larger than the
door jamb itself. This gap will be concealed by the door frame moulding. Now set the
door and frame into the space in the flat about 1 to $1\frac{1}{2}$ in. (2·5 to 3·75 cm.) away from
the flat.

Brace the door independently from the flat. In this way the door can be slammed
without the flat moving at all, and although the frame may move slightly, neither this
nor the gap between the two structures will be noticed from the auditorium.

It is often necessary to have a sash window on a set which can be opened and closed.
This is achieved by using the same principle as a normal sash window. The window
frame has runners between which the window can slide up and down. It is suspended

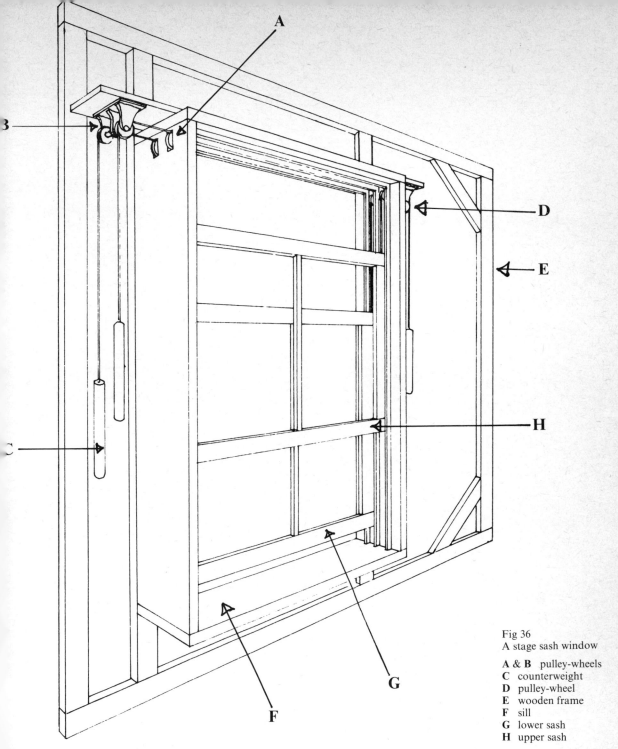

Fig 36
A stage sash window

A & B pulley-wheels
C counterweight
D pulley-wheel
E wooden frame
F sill
G lower sash
H upper sash

on two cords which go through pulleys in the top of the frame, then over another pulley about 6 in. (15 cm.) away from the outside of the frame, to keep the counter-weights, to which the other ends of the cords are attached, clear of the frame. These counterweights can be balanced to match the weight of the window frame if they are made of canvas bags containing sand, lead shot, or old nuts.

A further refinement (which becomes absolutely necessary if the piece has to be moved during a scene change) is to stretch a guide line of nylon down the back of the

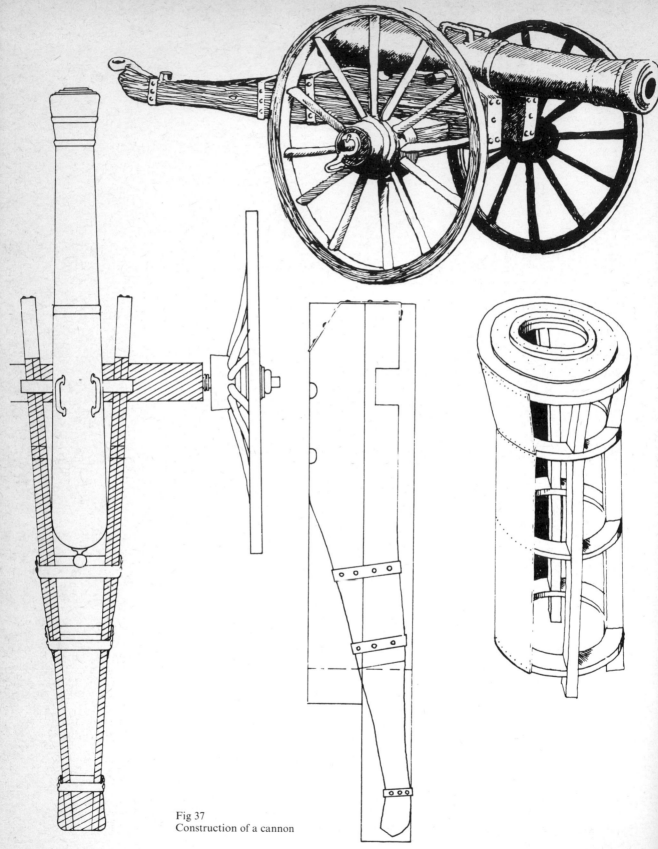

Fig 37
Construction of a cannon

flat parallel to the track of the moving counterweight. The counterweight bag can be fixed by a loosely fitting wire loop to this guide line, which will stop it from swinging and becoming unmanageable while moving.

6   Heavy wood and tubular constructions, and cast metal finishes   Example: a cannon

Strange as it may seem it is often necessary to have a cannon on stage especially during an opera, or even during a play such as *Mother Courage*. As a cannon is expensive to hire and impossible to find it is usually better to make one.

The cannon illustrated was made for a production of *Narrow Road to the Deep North*, and it was modelled on an eighteenth-century twelve-pounder. The construction is surprisingly easy; the most difficult part is obtaining a suitable pair of wheels. These can sometimes be found in rural areas, or borrowed from a cart or small wagon. Having begged, borrowed or found a pair of wheels, preferably mounted on an axle as this is difficult to construct, one can start building a box for it. The carriage will rest on this box, so it should be securely attached to the axle. It can be constructed from 6×1 in. (15×2.5 cm.) or 9×1 in. (22.5×2.5 cm.) timber, but old scaffold planks if they can be found are ideal as they are $1\frac{1}{4}$ to $1\frac{1}{2}$ in. (2.88 to 3.75 cm.) thick and usually 9 in. (22.5 cm.) wide. The carriage in the drawing needed two joined edge to edge to make up the width and also a double layer on the front part to make up the thickness. This second 'layer' was pared down to a flat wedge shape with a plane. The shape of the carriage was then drawn on the planks and cut out, and the second layer was nailed and glued to the first. Finally the two sides were bound together with welded metal straps bolted through the planks. These held the planks together and formed the basic shape of the carriage. Metal attachments were now added. They consisted of handles, hooks, and eye bolts. These were obtained from metal scrapyards, breakers' yards, and old disused farm machinery. Some of these had a practical use, such as the handles (which were the heavy cast iron handles of an old disused boiler). Other attachments were purely decorative. The frame of the carriage was now fixed to the axle box by means of joints cut into the sides of the carriage to fit snugly over the box, then glued and held with metal angle straps screwed to the carriage and axle box. The last thing was to burn the wood with a blow torch, as with the bench described above.

The barrel is a hollow construction made up of circular $\frac{3}{4}$ in. (1.88 cm.) plywood formers held together with four or five 'stringers' which are half lap jointed to the circular formers. These formers will make the cylindrical tapering shape of the barrel. The barrel has a wide domed base at the back and then tapers towards the muzzle where it flares slightly. The back dome can be built by gluing plywood discs, of gradually reducing circumference, on top of each other. The indentations are filled in with plaster of paris mixed with either size or emulsion medium to make it hard when it has set. The formers are now covered with sheets of skin ply cut to the width between the centres of the formers, and glued and tacked on. The moulding on the muzzle is also built up of different sized hollow circles of plywood which are rounded off with a rasp and filled with plaster, mixed as for the dome base. The mounting spindle can now be built. It should be a thick piece of dowel fixed through the barrel with enough projecting on either side to sit on the indentations prepared on the top of the carriage frame. On a real cannon there were usually two of these indentations to make different elevations of the gun possible.

The decorative rings should now be added to the barrel. They can either be formed by thin strips of skin ply glued in the correct places, or with pieces of felt impregnated with size; this method could also be used for the back half of the whole barrel which in the cannon illustrated is slightly thicker. When the size dries the felt has a very hard surface. The handles can either be made up from found bits or cut and shaped from a piece of $\frac{3}{4}$ in. (1.88 cm.) plywood. If the action of the play demands that the gun be dismantled or the barrel moved, it is better if the handles are real prefabricated items as they will have to be very securely attached to the barrel.

Once this stage is reached the whole barrel should be rounded, sanded, and finished. To obtain the texture of a cast object one can either coat the whole barrel with a thin

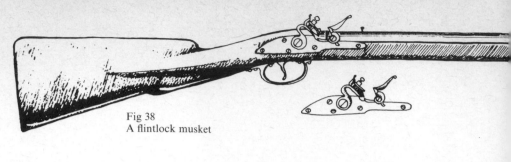

Fig 38
A flintlock musket

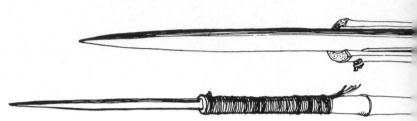

mixture of plaster and size, almost painting it on, or spread a thin mixture of resin and sawdust very thinly on to the surface. Whichever coating is used it should, while still tacky, be 'lifted' by touching it with a pad of cloth and pulling away; this will leave a rough texture all over the barrel. When this is dry it should be smoothed down all over with a medium glasspaper (sandpaper). This will give the slightly pitted appearance which cast metal objects have; although slightly more exaggerated than the real thing, this does not matter because it should look completely convincing from the auditorium. Now the whole barrel should be painted with a mixture of graphite powder and size, or graphite powder and emulsion medium. When this mixture is dry, the barrel should be burnished with a piece of smooth metal, e.g., the back of a spoon. If a blacker metal effect is required the surface can be covered with stove black. This can be applied with a brush and burnishes the coating, giving the same effect as that of an old cast iron, polished stove. If the barrel needs to look like bronze, a small amount of brass powder should be mixed with the graphite; this, when dry and unburnished, should be coated with a very thin glaze of green oxide coloured paint. When this is burnished the effect is totally convincing, giving an overall dull bronze glint with the greenish colour remaining in the pit marks of the texture and recesses of the moulding.

If you decide to use resin for the surface texture, a short cut can be taken by adding graphite, or graphite and bronze, to the resin and then burnishing this when dry—this will have exactly the same effect, but with the advantage of being much harder and more durable.

7 Fire arms Example: a flintlock musket

This can be made with a wooden butt and stock, and a metal or wooden barrel. The shape should be drawn out on a piece of wood at least $1\frac{1}{4}$ in. (2·88 cm.) thick and then fretworked out. It can be chiselled roughly to shape, then finished with a spokeshave or surform and rasp, and, finally, glasspaper (sandpaper). The barrel, either metal or dowel, is separately attached. A long groove, of the same circumference as the dowel or conduit tube to be used, should be carved into the top of the stock. Then the barrel piece should be laid into this groove. The woodwork should be finished before the barrel is attached. This is done by staining with a proprietary wood dye and then polishing it with either furniture wax or, quicker still, the paraffin wax of a normal candle. The barrel is now fixed by binding it to the stock tightly and neatly either with thin wire or felt glued and tacked tightly. This felt is then sized and, when dry, treated

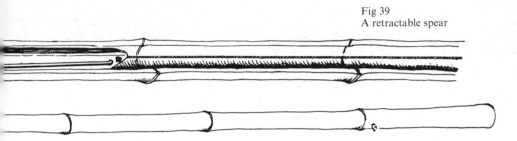

Fig 39
A retractable spear

with a mixture of metal powder and resin which can be smoothed and burnished when it has set. After drilling a small hole through the barrel near the base where a sight might be situated, a screw can be inserted which will hold barrel and stock securely together. The lock is slightly more complicated. It can be made by building up and welding found pieces, for instance the parts of an old clock, on to a base plate or fabricating such pieces out of thin metal. The base plate is now screwed to the stock in the correct position.

This is a reasonable method if only one musket is required, but if a number are needed it is best to cast a number of locks from a clay mould. These are best cast in resin mixed with a quantity of metal powder to give the colour required. They can be made as a solid piece with the base plate included. The whole can then be screwed to the stock and burnished. The trigger can be manufactured in the same way, or made up of a piece of thin metal bent to shape.

8 Retractable weapons Example: a spear

Trick weapons are often difficult to get hold of and so it is useful to know a simple way of making them. The spear illustrated is simple, cheap and also much quieter than the usual trick blade which often makes the awful noise of metal on metal when operated.

A hollow tube forms the shaft of the spear, and all the working parts must fit into this hollow space. The one illustrated was made of bamboo as this was in keeping with the play. It could be made equally well from aluminium or thin steel tube and then, if necessary, painted to look like wood. The divisions at the joints of the bamboo were removed by burning them out with a hot iron rod. The inside was then smoothed down with glasspaper (sandpaper) glued to a piece of dowelling. The blade was made next, out of hardwood. It should be made long enough so that at least half the length is inside the hollow shaft. The concealed half carries the spring and stop.

The blade should be shaped and made at least $\frac{1}{8}$ in. (0·32 cm.) thinner at its widest point than the inside of the shaft. This is necessary so that it can easily retract and allow the rubber spring to fit alongside it in the tube. The spring is of rubber, at least $\frac{1}{8}$ in. (0·32 cm.) square or, if this is not obtainable, a thin strip of heavy motor car tyre inner tube can be used. The base of the blade has two small holes drilled in it. To one is tied the end of a piece of very strong cord (fishing line is best). This should be threaded through a hole in the base of the shaft and drawn through to the top and tied through one of the holes in the blade. It is no easy job to thread this string through.

The best way is to thread a thin wire with an eye bent in it which will go through the hole, and push this up to the top of the shaft. Thread the cord through and draw it, by means of the wire, back through the hole at the base.

Now, attach the spring. This is a process of trial and error as it depends on the tension of the particular elastic used. Thread the elastic through the other hole in the base of the blade and knot it with a large knot on the other side of the hole. A figure of eight knot is best. When the elastic is stretched fully this knot should still be large enough not to slip through the hole. Now thread the elastic through a small hole drilled through the shaft as near to the top as possible. Pull the string stop through the hole in the base, drawing the blade into the shaft until the right amount of spear blade projects at the top. Tie the string.

The elastic must now be tensioned. The rubber should be drawn taut through the hole in the top of the shaft. The elastic pulls against the string stop. This will hold the blade in place, the string preventing it from falling out and the tension on the rubber preventing it from sliding back into the shaft. Now, marking the position of the rubber with a ball point pen at the point where it emerges from the hole, hold it firmly on this mark and push the blade into the shaft. If it does not go in reasonably easily slacken off the rubber slightly until it does and make a new mark. With a few adjustments the right tension on the elastic will be found. Now tie the elastic at the final mark in the same way as it was attached to the blade. To do this it may become necessary to slacken off the string stop to give enough room for manoeuvre, but first mark the string at its exit point. Now tie the string at its mark and the spear should retract without hurting when pressed point foremost into the flesh. It will then spring back when withdrawn giving, from the auditorium, the impression of going into and coming out of the unfortunate victim's body.

The spear can then be decorated as required.

Flowers and Foliage

CAROL LAWRENCE

It is not easy to generalize about making anything for the stage, especially the vege-
table matter; like everything else, it is a matter of circumstances. For one thing it
usually has the smallest budget, and for another thing it is usually the last to be thought
of as far as construction is concerned. It tends to be made, therefore, with whatever is
left over, or happens to be around at the time. Unless, of course, the show happens to
be *Jack and the Beanstalk*, and the greenery one of the main characters.

Sometimes it is more successful to make the supporting greenery quite haphazardly
at the last moment. A particular show forces you to work within its own style and
every show has its own clichés, no matter how clever you have tried to be. When you
have been working days and nights for a few weeks, and it is suddenly the last night
before opening, and you just remember that you have ninety leaves to make, you do
tend to pick up any old bit of material, and borrow some paint someone has mixed
for the floor, and make them all quickly with whatever else is around, and it all fits,
and that is important. If, on the other hand, someone has been given the job especially,
they often go away and do the job very carefully, and the result upon the stage looks
like candles on a birthday cake, and has to be bashed about to make it fit in with the
rest. Much the same thing often happens with hats when you are doing costume.

Before I describe how to make anything, I should make it clear that the methods
used may not be those of a professional theatrical prop maker, but rather those used
by people in rep. without the money to pay someone to do the job, and who often have
to 'get on with it', usually in the middle of the night, without a clue how to start.

In ideal circumstances, the very first thing to do is some research, as with anything
else on the stage. For example, there may be a certain kind of plant mentioned in the
text; if there is not, and it is a period play, you should look at photographs or paintings
of the period, and find out exactly what sort of flowers, in what sort of arrangements
they had in the drawing room, and what plants they were fond of having in the
conservatory, or climbing the walls. You should also find out what time of the year
it is when the action is taking place. It is no use making arrangements of daffodils
when the play is set in August, just because you happen to have some spare. Even the
time of day should be considered, as wide awake morning type daisies might look rather
strange in twilight. More important, you must remember what country the action is
taking place in. In other words, everything upon the stage must be part of the same
experience and picture. After all, you have presumably taken some trouble to find the
right clothes and furniture, so it would be a bit silly to make a laughable mistake with
the bits round the edges. A mistake in the smallest part can give the lie to the whole,
because there is always someone who will notice. So, first, research is important.

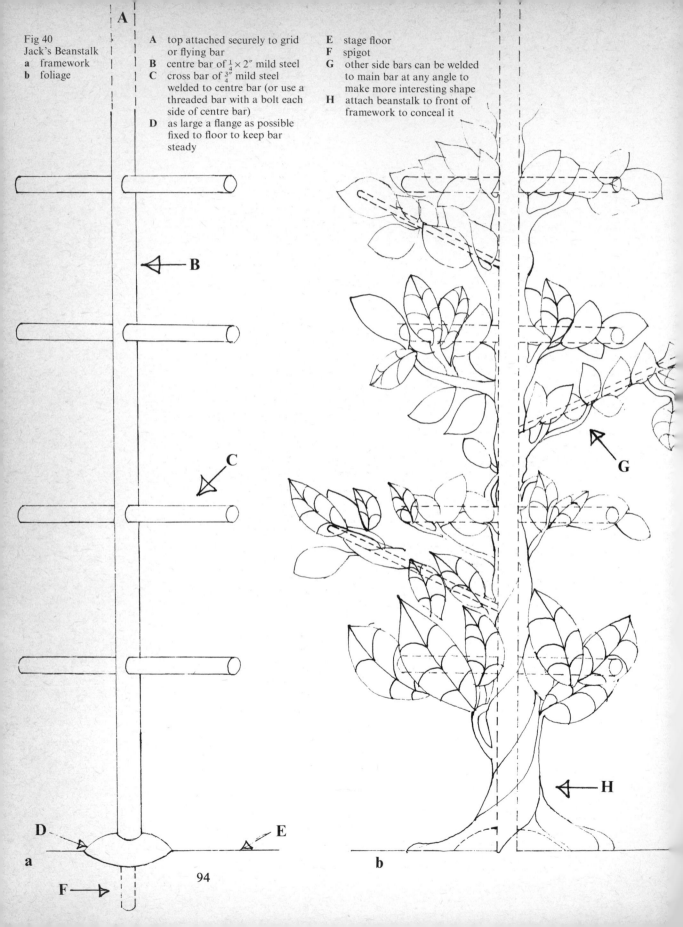

Fig 40
Jack's Beanstalk
a framework
b foliage

A top attached securely to grid or flying bar
B centre bar of $\frac{1}{4} \times 2''$ mild steel
C cross bar of $\frac{3}{4}''$ mild steel welded to centre bar (or use a threaded bar with a bolt each side of centre bar)
D as large a flange as possible fixed to floor to keep bar steady
E stage floor
F spigot
G other side bars can be welded to main bar at any angle to make more interesting shape
H attach beanstalk to front of framework to conceal it

Next, the choice of materials that you use, if you have a choice, should also fit in with the scenery, and the period in which it is set. Fibreglass plants might look strange in a Victorian room, but can look beautiful in another show where canvas would look old fashioned. This is not to say that you should use only materials available in the period in which the play is set, unless you really want to carry things to extremes. After a while you instinctively know which material will become something with the right 'feel' about it, and it is fun to use something different for each play, approaching each job as a different problem, rather than learning by heart that you always make leaves in such a way, and sticking to it grimly.

You should experiment without following any rules (except those on the glue tube), as long as you are absolutely certain in your mind of what you want to achieve. You might wonder why one should bother to make flowers, rather than getting real ones. Well, you could, apart from a theatre superstition about them, like wearing green, or whistling, but even disregarding that, they do not work well on the stage. The lights drain them, they wilt, and it is an awful bother for someone to keep replacing them. As with everything else, flowers undergo a strange metamorphosis on the stage, where something made will look real, and something real will look false. Real branches, and sometimes evergreen leaves, are another matter, but I will mention these later.

Even so, the best thing to do is to get a live example (or at least a photograph if it is something large or exotic and difficult to get) of what you want to make, and study it. Now, and this sounds very whimsy, you should look at the plant very hard, and try to discover exactly what it is that makes the plant what it is, and not another, and it is this quality that you try to reproduce. You do not get side-tracked, for example, by the exact number of petals on a chrysanthemum, but find out instead exactly what makes its 'chrysanthemumness', so that even if the stage were in semi-darkness, you would still know what it was, and not mistake it for a daisy. In other words, you get the essentials right, and forget about the biological trimmings, unless, of course, it is for a close-up in a film.

Most people (meaning audience) do not look at plants carefully anyway (except for gardeners who look for greenfly), but 'take in' shapes and textures without realizing it, and it is this that you must reproduce, perhaps in an abstract, or impressionistic way, but the truth none the less. If you can look upon a plant as a thing, and forget what it is called, the right material to use will suggest itself. Any plant or flower which is touched by an actor should obviously behave in the way that it would if real. This makes things slightly more complicated, but should follow as a matter of course if you have done all the right research and found the right material to use. An obvious example: poppies made from tissue paper or thin silk would handle in the right way, while poppies made from felt would look much too heavy as soon as they were handled. If an actor has to arrange flowers on stage, you can avoid the sound of lots of rustling paper by mixing some real foliage in with the bunch, and have the actor 'arrange' that.

If you take the actors as the point of focus (I say actors for simplicity, but it also means singers or dancers or performers in general), anything near them must be absolutely perfect, but going from them to the edges of the stage picture, objects can be more misty and suggested. This is a personal point of view and some people would disagree, but it is clearly pedantic to put every leaf upon a tree, when all you need is a suggestion of the right kind of tree for the audience to accept it, without looking too closely, and then to concentrate on the actors. They, after all, are what it's all about, and it is they the audience should come to see, not the pretty stage effects. Every object upon the stage should be put there either to help the performer to create the right world for the play, or to help him to do his job; anything there for its own sake is superfluous and should go.

Trees and shrubs

For the quickest and easiest tree of all, you just gather a large branch, or a small tree from a place where it is possible to steal or beg a tree. You can get dead or storm-felled

95

Fig 41
Frame for tree with small trunk

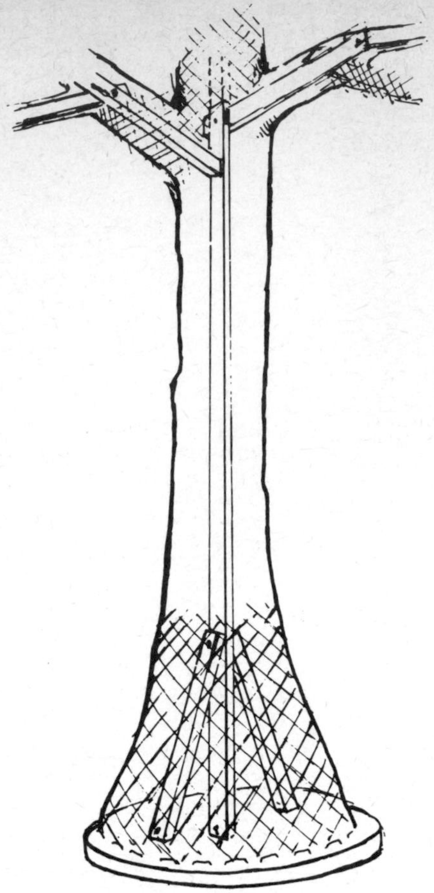

Fig 42
Frame for tree with larger trunk

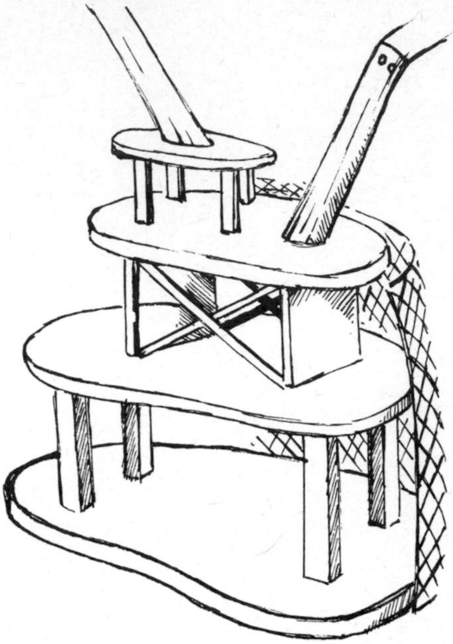

ones from parks, or branches from the local authority from trees they have trimmed from road sides. You must choose one with roughly the right shape for the tree you want to make, and with enough twigs to make it interesting. It must also be strong enough to stand up (with support) and be moved around a bit, because it is very upsetting to spend a long time dressing the tree with leaves only to have it crumple up on the first night.

If you cannot steal a spare tree from anywhere, you can make one by constructing a rough wooden framework then squashing wire mesh or chicken wire around it to give it its body. You can cover this in a variety of ways to get the effect you need, brown paper and glue, or canvas and size, or scrim dipped in plaster. If you have to reproduce a scale model of a tree exactly, you first take measurements of the trunk and branches, length not circumference. Then you reproduce these exactly by drawing them full size on the ground. Make a wooden framework to these dimensions, also on the ground, then stand it up and cover it in any of the ways described above. A frame for a tree with a small trunk (fig. 41) can be made as follows. Cut an irregular circle of strawboard or plywood for the base. Nail 2 × 1 in. (5 × 2·5 cm.) timber into the basic shape. To support this make a tripod of 2 × 1 in. (5 × 2·5 cm.) timber and nail it to the base and upright. Nail on as many branches as you need, in various thicknesses of wood. Staple chicken wire round the base, crush and mould it to the shape you want, wiring the wooden core so that it is firm. For a frame for a tree with a large trunk (fig. 42), cut irregular shapes of chipboard, strawboard or plywood, support them with a wooden framework, make wood branches and cover the whole thing with wire mesh.

Another way of making a tree is to start by winding strips of canvas dipped in size round and round the framework. When that is dry, you can stick on bits of foam or polystyrene cut roughly to shape, and filed down when fixed, to give the tree the right

96

thickness and bumps. Then cover it with a final layer of canvas and size, or plaster of paris, or gauze, depending upon how delicate the tree has to look. Then, of course, paint it the right colour. When you have the tree, you can cut the leaf shapes from canvas, paint them, and glue them on with Copydex or similar glue. If you cover them with emulsion medium after painting it will make them stiff and glossy.

Another method of making leaves is with fabric and fibreglass resin. You first find the right colour net (dress material sort). You could dye gauze or muslin, but obviously it takes longer, and anyway you can always vary the colour by painting with dye afterwards if necessary. Cut out the shape of leaves you want (you can do lots at the same time) then dip them into, or paint them with, resin to which a hardener has been added (directions are on the bottle), so they do not take weeks to dry. Then lay them on polythene sheets until they are ready. If you spread them on newspaper, it becomes part of the leaf, and takes ages to peel off. Before the leaves are completely dry you can, if you wish, bend them to make curved leaf shapes instead of flat. You can make lots of leaves very quickly this way, but it takes time to wire them all individually on the tree. Just make a small hole in the base of the leaf, and attach it to the branch with any fine wire so that it doesn't show. The effect will be slightly translucent and rather delicate, and ideal when a 'poetic' tree is needed.

If you want a densely-foliaged tree, you can use the same method, but make a sort of collage instead of each separate leaf. Just cut the shape of a clump of leaves from net and dip it in the resin; then stick a few leaf shapes of dyed calico or net on here and there while it is still wet, to give it some depth. Then wire the whole thing on a branch. To add more depth you can vary the colour, having the individual leaves a lighter colour than the base.

Unless you absolutely have to have a whole tree, i.e., it is specified in the text, or it has to be used for climbing, or some other purpose, or is a designer's whim, it is probably much better to get away with suggesting a tree, by using just a branch from above, or the side, and 'filling in' on the floor and backcloth with lighting effects. These can be made by using a special light for the job, or you can just put 'artistic' blotches with aniline dye on coloured cinemoid, and put it in front of a few strategically placed lights.

Another way to make tree foliage is to use feathers. It sounds bizarre, but can look quite natural. You can get chicken feathers quite cheaply wholesale from chicken farms or feather agencies. You can also, of course, get other kinds if they would suit the tree you are making better, but they will probably be more expensive. First you have to dump the feathers in a large tub of boiling dye, which should kill the lice as well as making them the right colour. Spread them on sheets of newspaper to dry and then they can be stuck on. You will probably need a framework on which to stick them to put upon the tree. For this, use shapes of wire mesh or chicken wire, covering it with paper or calico or canvas, stuck with size to fill in the holes in the mesh, then stick the feathers on with Copydex or Scotch Contact until it is covered. It is better to arrange it so that the feathers overlap the framework and each other, or it looks too heavy, and spoils the effect that you are using them for.

Some branches with leaves can be preserved with wax, but you have to experiment with this as the plant might die at the vital moment. Just melt lots of candles and keep the wax warm and liquid and then coat the foliage carefully with the wet wax.

If you need to make any sort of long leaves, for example, for things like Victorian pot plants, or, to go to extremes, jungle-type ferns, it is very simple, using cane and canvas for the large leaves, and cane and calico for the smaller ones. Just cut a piece of cane (garden type) to the length of the leaf you want, and split it to make it more bendy and pliable. Then cut two pieces of canvas in the shape of the leaf, put lots of glue (whatever is handy) on the canvas, put the cane on one piece, then sandwich it with the other, and thump it down hard. When it is dry, cut the edges of the leaf down to the cane in fronds, or in whatever way you need to make the leaf right. Then paint it the right colour, and when it is dry, you can paint it with emulsion medium if the leaves need to look glossy.

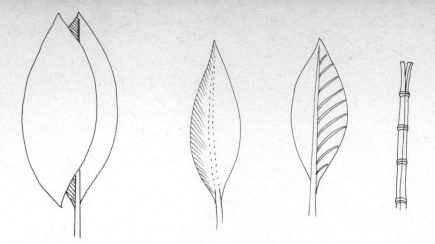

Fig 43
Constructing large leaves

If you need to make leaves with veins showing, cut one side of the leaf from canvas, then glue it, and put the cane in the centre, and glue string to the canvas to make the veins. Then cover this side with something lighter, such as gauze or paper, and press it down hard to make the string veins stand out. If you want a plant with very curly leaves, you can do the same thing, but use wire for the centre support instead of cane, then you can bend the leaf as you wish when it is dry. You must be careful to use the right size wire for the amount of bendiness you need. It is probably better to make small and medium size pot plants this way. You can also use the same method for the leaves of flowers, but two layers of material would probably be too bulky. Cover the wire at the back with a strip of the same material, and leave the wire longer for a stem, and cover that too.

32 *The Tulip Tree*, Haymarket Theatre, 1962. Photo: Angus McBean. The trees change from spring to summer between acts

To make difficult trees like yews, and also hedges, if you cannot avoid it, which is best, the easiest way is to use bits of the real thing. Make sure that they are evergreen and will last for a while, or ensure that they can be replaced daily. Spraying with emulsion glaze will make them last longer. First you have to make a framework. For the tree you use a hollow tube, of metal if you can afford it because it will be stronger. Or, if you cannot, a cardboard one will do, the sort that carpets are wrapped around in stores are usually very strong. Into the tube you drill holes in the right sort of places to make it look like a real tree when you do the next thing, which is to simply put the real branches into the holes. You have, of course, to build the tube up a little, and paint it and texture it to make it trunk-like. You may also have to trim the branches off to make it a believable shape. The same principle is also good for trees which must change seasons during the course of the play; it is simply a matter of changing the branches.

For the hedges, you make a framework of wood and cover it with wire mesh on the sides that show. Fill as many of the holes as you need to until it looks like a hedge (you may need a great many), then trim it. Stems of laurel, or privet, or even holly, which won't look like a holly hedge on stage, will last best. In one play I was working on a hedge had to grow between one scene and the next, as in both scenes it was seen in the process of being cut. This was done very simply by attaching a piece of 3×1 in. ($7 \cdot 5 \times 2 \cdot 5$ cm.) pine deal to the back of the framework with hinges. Into this holes were drilled, and they were filled with long pieces of the foliage used for the hedge. When the moment arrived for the hedge to grow, the 'loaded' wood was flapped up and pinned securely.

Three different ways of making shrubs are illustrated in fig. 46. The one in fig. 46a has trunk and branches of metal rod backed with fine metal mesh. The leaves can be foil or plastic. Fig. 46b shows a shrub cut out of a sheet of cobex (fireproof perspex) covered with grey scene gauze and painted with green and brown emulsion. It is fixed

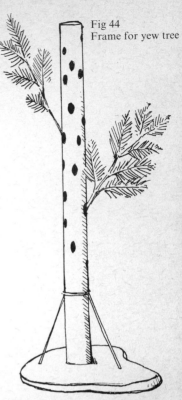

Fig 44
Frame for yew tree

99

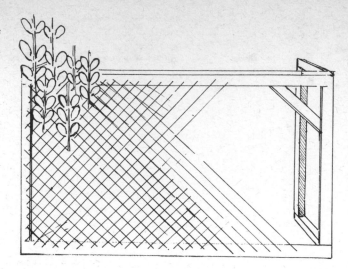

Fig 45
Frame for hedge

through a small polystyrene mound to a metal plate. The framework of the shrub in fig. 46c is a cane loop with three cane stiffeners mounted on a plywood base. The loop is covered in fine garden netting and fabric leaves in various colours attached.

Creepers

For the sort of creepers that climb over houses, just bind rope, or paper rope, with strips of material, winding leaves, and flowers if you need them, in as you go. Paper rope can be painted with dye to make it the right colour. It is best to make the creeper the right size before binding etc., and to wire side stems to the main stem.

For jungle-type creepers, you can really have fun. Just dip rope, which you can unravel a bit to make it fibrous, or drape with plumber's hemp (a coarse yellowish fibre used by plumbers and sold in hanks by ironmongers and hardware stores), in plaster and hang it up to drip into shape. You can use brown plaster, or paint when dry.

Fig 46
Different types of shrub

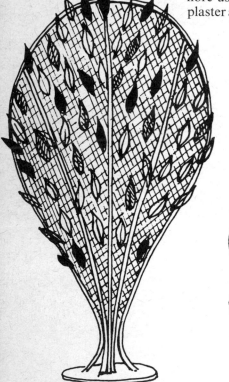

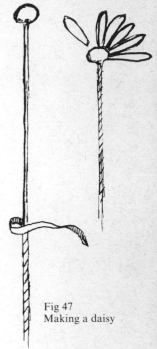

Fig 47
Making a daisy

Flowers

First, if it is anything at all difficult, daffodils for example, buy plastic ones. They are usually very good, but if there is anything unnatural about them, it is usually the colour, and you can easily change that. For the best effect mix them with something real, like evergreen leaves, or the sorts of ferns which you can buy from the florist. You can, of course, make daffodils from crêpe paper or material, but they are very fiddly and take some time, and you have to be very good at it to achieve a good effect.

Roses made from tissue paper can look lovely. They can be stuck, but I sew mine. First you fold a large rectangle of tissue until it is a small one, and cut out a rose petal shape; this way you can make lots at the same time. Then roll up a long strip of tissue for the centre, and sew the petals around this until the flower is big enough. You can do the same thing using fabric, but you have to paint each petal with millinery varnish or felt stiffener to stiffen it, then shape it around the end of an iron to curve it, so it obviously takes much longer.

Daisy-type flowers are easy too. Just bind a length of fine wire tightly with a strip of green material—you can bind pre-made leaves up the stem as you go—then stick a small piece of foam rubber on the tip and bind that too. Then sew petals of white, or coloured, gauze around it. Most flowers can be made this way, and on the whole I find

Fig 48
Making a rose

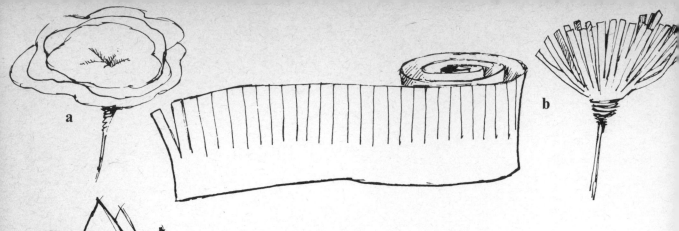

Fig 49
Making exaggerated flowers

sewing easier than sticking, as I usually manage to glue the petals to my fingers and nothing else, and it is important to keep the result clean.

Some flowers may look difficult, but can be made by using a seemingly strange material. I made a chrysanthemum once by gluing and wiring wood shavings on to a wooden knitting needle, using the nob at the top as the centre of the flower, and dyeing it the right colour afterwards. It looked surprisingly real. With made flowers it is often the stem that looks wrong, so it is important to bind them tightly until they are the right thickness, or cover them with a thin rubber tube, or you can try using dried stems dyed the right colour. It is also worthwhile looking in flower shops for dried plants that can be useful for flower centres, or find your own in nearby hedgerows, if you have the time. It is very useful to have a collection which you can use when you need it, and, as I said before, anything can become anything. Dried grasses are useful to mix with prop flowers in vase arrangements, and plants like honesty and dyed pampas grass are good for Victorian and Edwardian plays.

For most flowers, you can go mad with tissue paper, or crêpe paper, or felt. There are plenty of books on this subject, so I am sure that it is not really necessary to say much about it here. They can all be made by wiring together layers of paper which have been cut in various ways. For rounded-petalled flowers, cut large irregular circles of crêpe paper, tissue paper or other suitable cloth, wire them together in the centre, then wind the wire round the outside at the centre (fig. 49a). To make a daisy type of flower cut a strip of paper or felt, fringe it and roll and wind wire round the base (fig. 49b). To make large-petalled flowers cut crêpe paper across the grain, then mould the petals to make them curved and wire them together round the bottom (fig. 49c).

Lastly, plants for pantomime, farce, or anything that has to be funny. Usually these have to have much harder wear than other sorts, and therefore have to be strongly made, which means very strong thread, or very strong glue. It also usually means making something slightly exaggerated and can be more fun than making realistic flowers, as you can usually leave out the difficult parts of them. You can make very flamboyant flowers from dyed feathers, though you have to be careful that the result does not look like parrots on sticks. To make anything with really giant petals, or leaves like the ones for Jack's beanstalk, you have to cut them from material, then wire them around the edge, and sometimes up the centre as well to support them. Although the shape of 'joke' flowers, etc., can be exaggerated, I think that the colour should be controlled. Purple poppies with pink leaves might look silly, or other-worldly, rather than funny. But, of course, it all depends on the show, like everything else that is made, which is where I began, so there I had better end.

There is a section in the introduction about fireproofing, but perhaps I should mention here that any of the things I have described, if made of an inflammable material, should be sprayed with some fire-proofing substance before it goes near the stage. There is one called Albi-clear for the paper flowers; it has a tendency to make things look shiny, so if this matters you should substitute fabric.

Jewellery and Decoration

ELIZABETH MONTGOMERY

Jewellery and decoration can add an important element to costume, and though the approach to their design for the stage has not altered very much in the last few decades the number of new techniques and products available is always increasing and their quality improving.

Styles in jewellery have varied so much over the centuries that it is only possible to touch on a few of the possibilities here. If these embellishments are to be exciting as well as appropriate the designer will need perhaps more visual imagination than for any other branch of prop making. Because of this the methods suggested here are intended to stimulate the reader's own inventions. It is not possible to make any set rules; often a flash of inspiration will suggest the right materials for certain effects. How to put them together is nearly always a matter of common sense, given a few basic techniques.

There is no lack of historical evidence when it comes to finding out how things should look. Jewellery has always been a status symbol and for centuries it was an integral part of the commissioned portrait whether of royalty, the aristocracy or, more recently, the flourishing bourgeoisie. It is in giving physical form to this visual representation that the problems start, in finding the materials and objects to give the right interpretation and avoiding making things over-decorated and fussy. In general it is safe to say that jewellery and decoration for the stage should be slightly larger than life, and rather simplified and broadened in design if they are to be effective.

Sometimes, especially when one is working on very early periods, simpler methods and materials are more lively and successful than the more sophisticated. If the new resins, plastics or synthetic rubbers are used the result can easily look too perfect, and machine-made. If you use less modern materials and an individual approach there will be an appropriate roughness and unevenness.

On the stage it is important to avoid glitter. Theatre lighting makes everything more brilliant and reflected light from untreated metal or stones can be most distracting. In any case until the eighteenth century it seems that stones were very seldom cut to give the brilliance they have today. Anything new which is put on the stage without treatment or breaking down tends to look cheap or much too new and experiment will show that you need considerably more 'antiquing' than you think. It must be done with the greatest care so that the result doesn't look messy or dirty, but worn and aged. The basic colour, which should be a little more subdued than you would expect, should be applied first and then the recessed areas darkened. The most suitable colours to use are black, khaki, brown and grey.

There are various ways of antiquing. The finished jewellery can be rubbed with black or brown shoe polish, well worked in so that it doesn't come off on the hands or costume; the advantage of this method is that it mellows the shine without killing it altogether. Careful spraying from an aerosol can is another way, but it is difficult to control and the range of colours available is limited. You can get a small spray gun which will spray any kind of paint, so that you can mix your own colour and texture. For small things a mouth spray works well. More controlled effects can be achieved by painting with acrylics, fabric or oil paints, but this method is, of course, considerably slower. A satisfactory way of killing too much shine is to spray on a matt paint which is near the basic colour of the stone or metal; the latter can be rubbed down with fine emery paper before spraying.

It is a good idea to make a collection of materials and objects which may be useful. These might include: canvas, thick, and thin felt for mounting and backing, plastic wood, alabastine, plaster of paris, size crystals, different kinds of glues, paints, varnishes and glazes, linen thread, strong needles and thimbles, milliners' pins and flat wire; braids, jewels, buttons, studs, beads, heavy lace, pearls, cabuchons and sequins; hardware items like small cogwheels (plastic or metal), rubber tubing and stripping, small padlocks, all thicknesses and kinds of wire, eyelets and washers; miscellaneous items such as leather, shells, pieces of polystyrene, balsa wood, cotton or wool balls, Christmas tree decorations, leather bootlaces, paperclips, pebbles, corks, broken pieces of tiles, and coloured glass—the list could be almost limitless. Neofol, obtainable from art stores, Supertoe (made for shoe toecaps), and in the United States Sculpt metal, are all useful products.

Sometimes you may need many repeats of identical pieces, for instance military insignia or plaques for helmets if you have an army on the stage. These can be modelled in clay, or plasticine, a mould made and then a cast taken in latex rubber or any other suitable material (see chapter on Moulding and Casting). The casts can then be painted, covered in metal foil, or fabric (velvet, for instance), and decorated with studs or broken down sequins. Individual pieces can be modelled direct in plastic wood, Neofol, or Sculpt metal, or carved from polystyrene, balsa wood or, if you are very skilful, from hard wood.

There are as many ways of designing and making crowns or coronets as there are styles of production or costume: they may have to be realistic reproductions of an original or abstract symbols of royalty; in either case it is vital that they should not look ridiculous, unless, of course, they are intended to do so. Nothing makes an actor look a bigger fool than a crown that falls down to his ears or perches on top of his head. So always start by making a cardboard or paper template and fit and refit it until the actor looks suitably regal; get the correct size, height and angle and then work out the design so that the join fits with the decoration. Once the template is right the crown can be cut and made in whatever material fits the production and your pocket. Brass crowns look very good but they are expensive as not many people are able to do their own metal work. It usually means finding a metal worker, giving him your template, and deciding with him what he can use for decoration. Ready-made brass leaves, bosses, and fleurs de lis may occasionally be found at antique markets. Failing this decorations may have to be made from plastic leaves and flowers. Don't forget to ask for holes to be drilled round the base of the crown so that a padding of felt, velvet or foam rubber can be sewn in to prevent the metal from slipping or hurting the actor's head; of course, the head fitting must be slightly big to allow for this.

The cheapest way to make a crown is simply to strengthen the basic template. Join it up and put it on a head block (if you haven't got one make a padded shape to represent a head and put the crown on that). Glue some flat millinery wire up the centres of the taller decorations, then thicken it with gummed brown paper, the kind used for packing up parcels; it should be stuck on in small pieces, making sure that it is adhering firmly, in as many layers as seem necessary. Alternatively you can do the same thing with papier-mâché, using newspaper or sugar paper and a cold water paste, keeping the work as dry as possible. Make sure that while it is setting it does not twist out of shape. When it is dry the edges should be trimmed off and bound with the

Fig 50
Crowns
a correct fit
b too small and splayed
c too large

Fig 51
Constructing a crown
a template
b flat hat wire behind leaves
c join
d padding

a

b   c   d

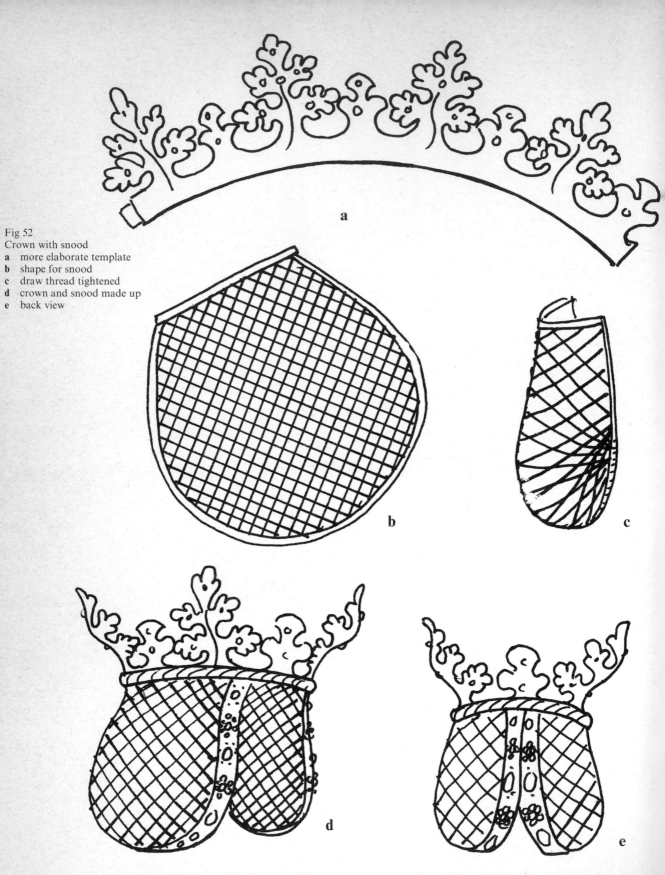

Fig 52
Crown with snood
a more elaborate template
b shape for snood
c draw thread tightened
d crown and snood made up
e back view

same paper as used in the making. The crown can then be painted and decorated to suit the production. Another method is to cut the shape from the template in buckram or canvas and to sew a hat wire all round the bottom edge and a flat wire up the centre of the taller decorations. Another way is to cut the design in two layers of felt, put flat millinery wire down the centre of the leaves on one layer and then glue the other layer on top. When the glue is dry paint the crown with hot size, soaking it well. When it has almost dried the designs can be pushed gently into shape and moulded with the finger from the back to give the relief effect. The crown can then be joined up round the head block and the leaves finally bent into position. When it is all completely dry a metal ring or sized thick gold cord can be fitted round the base. This should then be padded. The same procedure can be followed with Supertoe, which comes with a special solution which softens and makes it malleable, although when it is set it is very hard and strong. When you have made your shape it can be covered with metal foil, tissue or lurex, or simply painted and decorated any way you choose. You can add a snood, which is made like this: cut a shape in net or make it from braid; bind the top edge; bind round the shaped edge and run a draw thread through it (fig. 52a); tighten the draw thread to make a bag for the hair (fig. 52b). The snood can then be glued or stuck into the crown (fig. 52c).

The type of crown in fig. 53 is made as follows. Cut a buckram base to fit round the head. Cut a circle of red velvet lined with vilene, pleat it and glue it into the base. Take two strips of gold braid decorated with cords and jewels, line the strips with canvas, placing a flat millinery wire in between the canvas and the braid, then join the strips in the centre to make a cross shape and glue them inside the base. Make the leaf ornaments of sized felt with a gold braid edge glued on, and glue these inside the base between the strips. The finial can be a polystyrene ball with a hole in the middle or even a cotton wool ball like those used in Christmas decorations, and some artificial flower stamens can be stuck into the centre.

It is important always to choose materials and fabrics which suit the period and

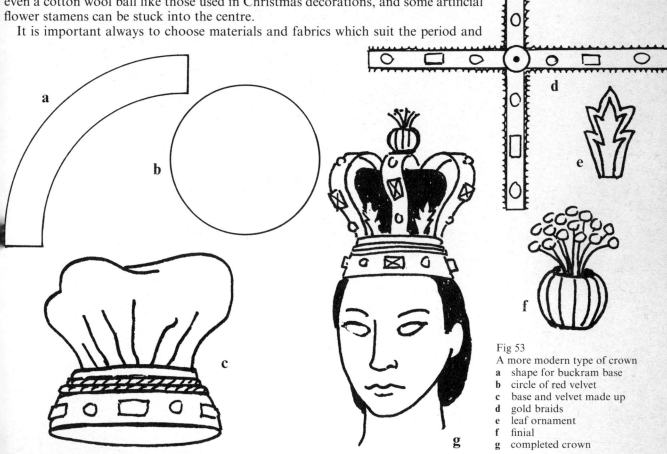

Fig 53
A more modern type of crown
a   shape for buckram base
b   circle of red velvet
c   base and velvet made up
d   gold braids
e   leaf ornament
f   finial
g   completed crown

107

Fig 54
Primitive brooch
a scrolls on felt base
b cross section

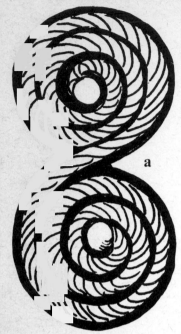

style of the production. For instance, for plays like *Macbeth* or *King Lear*, heavy rough materials work well while for the eighteenth century it is right to use something more delicate and elegant.

Primitive and archaic

The ornaments of these times were usually heavy with broad and often coarse detail, made in gold and silver, iron or bronze; they were seldom jewelled, but sometimes semi-precious stones, such as turquoise and agate, were used.

To get the effect of iron, mix a very little silver powder with black paint, and burnish or glaze it when it is completely dry. Alternatively the object can be painted black, varnished and, while it is still wet, a little silver powder can be sprinkled over it. To produce a bronze effect, use the same process with dark brown paint and bronze powder. Your collection should be able to supply you with most of the materials which are useful for this period: thick felt or leather for foundations (the felt can be soaked in size, and twisted into shape, as can Supertoe). For decorating costumes you can use rope and cord of different thicknesses, nuts, bolts, metal scouring pads and cloths, washers, rivets, and other hardware, metal buttons and studs. Balsa wood and polystyrene can be used for carving. The brooch in fig. 54 can be made by drawing out the shape on felt and marking the scrolls, then gluing firm cord over the marking and finishing the raw ends with a metal stud. (It is always wise to reinforce gluing with some stitches of linen thread.) Spray or paint the finished brooch to look like iron, red gold, copper or silver, and 'antique' it a good deal. A brooch for Glen Byam Shaw's *King Lear* at Stratford on Avon was made by carving a large rough stone out of polystyrene and painting and glazing it to look like a rough turquoise. The setting was made by cutting a piece of thick card the same shape as the stone, but a little bigger, building up the edge with one or two layers of card to form a nest for the stone. A large safety pin was wired to the back, and then the whole setting was covered with thin black leather, glued and tooled on, and turned over the back and glued down. The whole setting was then sprayed lightly with bronze paint. Finally the stone was glued into place in its nest. (See chapter on Hand Props and Soft Props for notes on the kind of glues to use with polystyrene.)

Archaic jewellery, worn by the ancient Greeks and Etruscans, is usually made from pure gold and is rather more sophisticated in design. The necklace in fig. 56, which is a copy of one in the British Museum, was made as follows. Plaques were modelled in Neofol, bent over to form loops at the top. The plaques were then mounted on felt, for strength, and strung on a leather thong. The beads are metal, but could equally well be plastic, china or painted wood. They are hung below the plaques by leather thongs

Fig 55
Brooch for *King Lear*
a card shape
b cross section of completed
brooch

34 Jewellery made from a great variety of materials in *Antony and Cleopatra*, the RSC production at the Aldwych Theatre, 1973. Photo: Sophie Baker

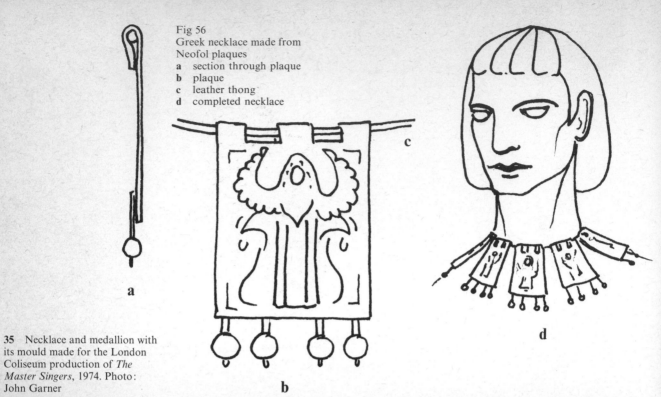

Fig 56
Greek necklace made from
Neofol plaques
a section through plaque
b plaque
c leather thong
d completed necklace

35 Necklace and medallion with
its mould made for the London
Coliseum production of *The
Master Singers*, 1974. Photo:
John Garner

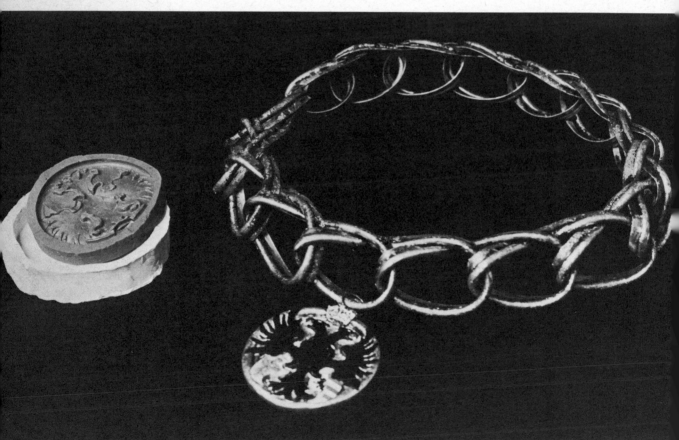

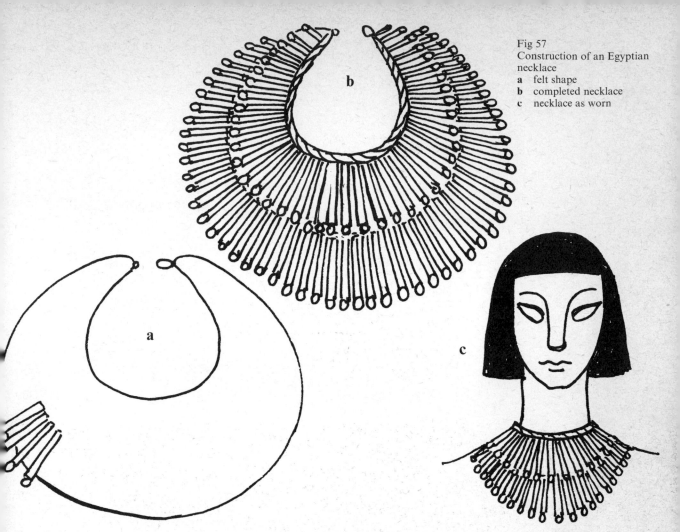

Fig 57
Construction of an Egyptian
necklace
a felt shape
b completed necklace
c necklace as worn

glued on between the two layers. The ancient Egyptians used a lot of wood, reeds and beads. Uncooked macaroni, thin bamboo, wooden, glass and plastic beads are useful for creating jewellery of this period. To make an Egyptian necklace, cut a felt shape to lie around the base of the neck and flat on the chest. Make a heavy knot in some linen thread or fine cord and drop on a turquoise blue bead. Pass the thread through a strip of bamboo or macaroni which has been cut to a suitable length and attach it to the collar. Repeat the process until the necklace is complete, starting with the bottom row. Finish with a cord at the neck and a button and loop fastening. Wooden curtain rings make good bracelets.

Gothic and Renaissance

As time went on work on personal adornment became more elaborate and the detail finer. Prop makers who like elaborate detail and decoration will enjoy themselves more and more as they approach the fifteenth century, by which time men and women were very ornately dressed with collars, chains, baldrics, jewelled coifs, elaborate belts, earrings, pendants, bracelets, brooches, and rings, all made with gold, silver, pearls, rough cut stones, etc. Costume details were tasselled and fringed and heraldic emblems were particularly popular.

To make a baldric, first cut a canvas or felt shape to fit the wearer. Cover it with coloured material or metal tissue (or simply use felt of the right colour, or paint the canvas). Edge the baldric with braid or cord and decorate it with studs or buttons or plastic mouldings. Tassels, bells or wooden balls can be hung on the lower edge.

Fig 58
Necklace made from macaroni and beads

111

Fig 59
Construction of a baldric

a & b two views of basic shape
c completed baldric
d baldric for carrying a sword
e baldric for decoration

Up until the second half of the fifteenth century the designs were flowing and gothic, but by the time of the Tudors the square broadness and heavy ornate decoration of the architecture and furniture began to have an influence on the costume decoration and jewellery. On the continent of Europe the Renaissance style appeared quite a lot earlier. Your collection should provide what you need for this period. Metal foils, gold and lurex tissues, Neofol, Sculpt metal, elaborate buttons, bosses, fine and coarse metallic cords, imitation stones, shells, pearls, braids, rubber tubing, gas pipes, door stops and rubber-covered electric flex can all be brought into use. Modelling and carving can also be used for this period.

36 The Canning Jewel. Victoria & Albert Museum

113

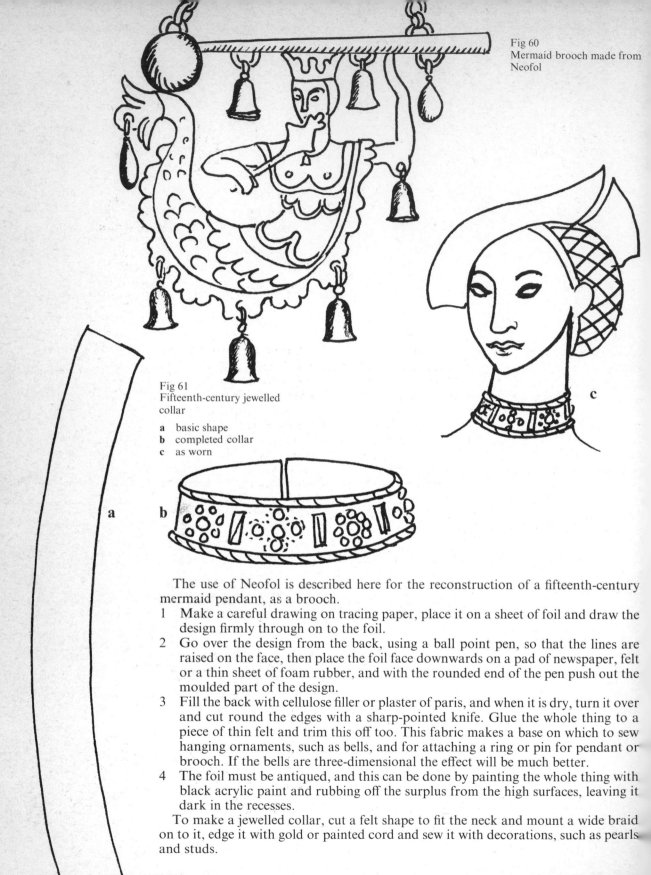

Fig 60
Mermaid brooch made from
Neofol

Fig 61
Fifteenth-century jewelled
collar

a basic shape
b completed collar
c as worn

The use of Neofol is described here for the reconstruction of a fifteenth-century mermaid pendant, as a brooch.

1 Make a careful drawing on tracing paper, place it on a sheet of foil and draw the design firmly through on to the foil.

2 Go over the design from the back, using a ball point pen, so that the lines are raised on the face, then place the foil face downwards on a pad of newspaper, felt or a thin sheet of foam rubber, and with the rounded end of the pen push out the moulded part of the design.

3 Fill the back with cellulose filler or plaster of paris, and when it is dry, turn it over and cut round the edges with a sharp-pointed knife. Glue the whole thing to a piece of thin felt and trim this off too. This fabric makes a base on which to sew hanging ornaments, such as bells, and for attaching a ring or pin for pendant or brooch. If the bells are three-dimensional the effect will be much better.

4 The foil must be antiqued, and this can be done by painting the whole thing with black acrylic paint and rubbing off the surplus from the high surfaces, leaving it dark in the recesses.

To make a jewelled collar, cut a felt shape to fit the neck and mount a wide braid on to it, edge it with gold or painted cord and sew it with decorations, such as pearls and studs.

114

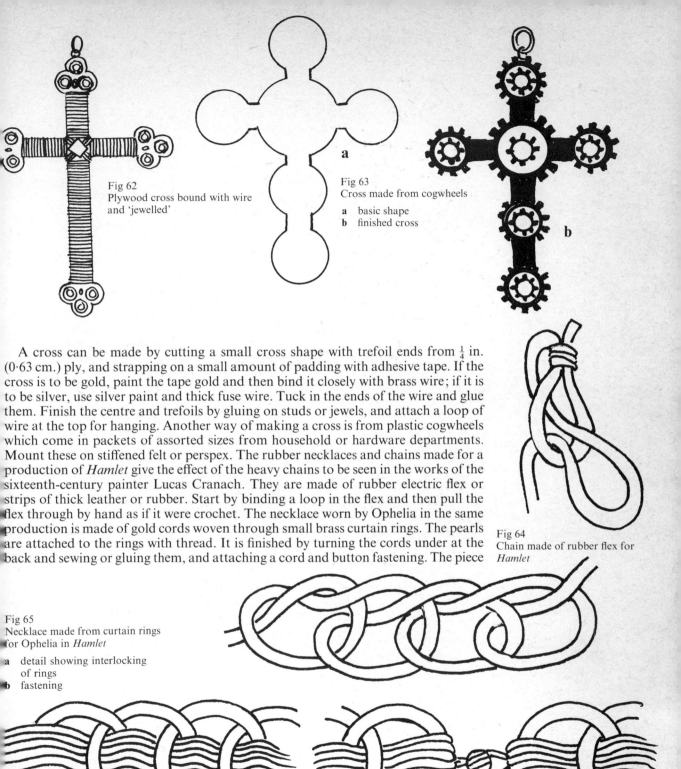

Fig 62
Plywood cross bound with wire
and 'jewelled'

Fig 63
Cross made from cogwheels

a basic shape
b finished cross

A cross can be made by cutting a small cross shape with trefoil ends from $\frac{1}{4}$ in. (0·63 cm.) ply, and strapping on a small amount of padding with adhesive tape. If the cross is to be gold, paint the tape gold and then bind it closely with brass wire; if it is to be silver, use silver paint and thick fuse wire. Tuck in the ends of the wire and glue them. Finish the centre and trefoils by gluing on studs or jewels, and attach a loop of wire at the top for hanging. Another way of making a cross is from plastic cogwheels which come in packets of assorted sizes from household or hardware departments. Mount these on stiffened felt or perspex. The rubber necklaces and chains made for a production of *Hamlet* give the effect of the heavy chains to be seen in the works of the sixteenth-century painter Lucas Cranach. They are made of rubber electric flex or strips of thick leather or rubber. Start by binding a loop in the flex and then pull the flex through by hand as if it were crochet. The necklace worn by Ophelia in the same production is made of gold cords woven through small brass curtain rings. The pearls are attached to the rings with thread. It is finished by turning the cords under at the back and sewing or gluing them, and attaching a cord and button fastening. The piece

Fig 64
Chain made of rubber flex for
Hamlet

Fig 65
Necklace made from curtain rings
for Ophelia in *Hamlet*

a detail showing interlocking
of rings
b fastening

from *Gloriana* shows the solidity of the sixteenth-century style. The miniature is made from a reproduction framed with a felt ring, set with paste jewels and stuck in a moulded surround. The chains are cord.

From the sixteenth century on it is much more difficult to improvise, because of the small scale and the skilful techniques involved. It is also more possible to buy inexpensive pieces which can be adapted and broken down to look very passable on the stage.

Seventeenth century
The craze for elaborate jewellery seems to have been in abeyance for a time and, of course, the Puritans considered it to be very sinful stuff. But even before the Puritans decoration relied more on ribbons and laces than on jewellery, although stones were set in the middle of ribbon rosettes and the women were very fond of pearls, long strings tucked into the bodice or waist, and chokers. These are much in evidence in the paintings of Peter Lely and Vandyke. The men wore earrings and rings on their fingers but not necklaces, chains or brooches. There is really nothing at this time which needs any special invention.

Eighteenth century
This was a period of much embroidery. Men wore rings and brooches to pin back their ruffles and their buttons and shoe buckles were jewelled. Women wore jewels in their hair, necklaces, pendants, brooches, earrings and rings on their fingers. All these were gold or silver set with diamonds and other precious stones, and they were very delicately and elaborately made.

Some of the effect of intricacy can be achieved by using heavy guipure or macramé lace, cutting out the motifs and piecing them together for necklaces and bracelets and mounting them for earrings and tiaras. When they are assembled they must be stiffened with felt stiffener (obtainable from milliner's suppliers), sprayed with gold or

37 'Elizabethan' brooch made for the London Coliseum production of *Gloriana*, 1966. Photo: John Garner

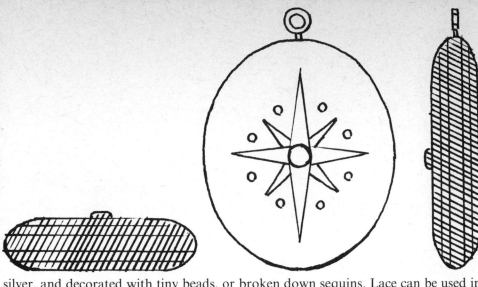

Fig 66
Victorian locket made from layers
of thin plywood

silver, and decorated with tiny beads, or broken down sequins. Lace can be used in the same way to make settings for stones.

Embroidery on coats and waistcoats or on military uniforms looks very good if it is made by applying a heavy lace with a bold pattern, such as the macramé used for tablecloths and the bottoms of blinds. It should either be dyed to match the cloth of the garment or, if the embroidery is supposed to be metallic, it can be dyed gold or grey. It should then be either sewn or stuck on to the garment, painted with colour or dry-brushed with gold or silver. For very elaborate costumes it can be decorated with jewels, beads, sequins, small buttons or studs, even brass paper clips can look effective. An appliqué of thin felt cut in elaborate patterns looks even richer if one or two layers are superimposed in diminishing sizes and in different shades. Leaves, for example, can be made with increasingly lighter shades of green. Flowers can be sewn only in the middle, leaving the petals to curl up.

The plastic decorations used on furniture, mentioned earlier, can be drilled with small holes and sewn on to coats and waistcoats. Mounted on felt, they make good brooches and earrings. This sort of decoration overlapped into the early part of the nineteenth century, but changed towards the forties into the style we now think of as Victorian.

The Victorian period

Lockets were very popular in this period. They were often worn on velvet ribbons and held miniatures, photographs or twists of hair, sometimes exposed to view and sometimes locked away inside. The Victorians also wore jet, enamel, painted ebony, elaborately carved ivory, and cameos as well as pinchbeck chains, small watches and chatelaines. It is difficult and time-consuming to make these things but they can be hired from costumiers or even from antique dealers. Cheap imitations can be bought and improved upon. Certain things can, of course, be made if hiring or buying is impractical, or if the play demands a special approach. Quite an acceptable locket, for example, can be made out of plywood or balsa wood. Cut the shape in $\frac{1}{2}$ in. (1·25 cm.) ply, then build up on both sides with one or two layers of $\frac{1}{4}$ in. (0·63 cm.) ply, cut in diminishing sizes. Glue them all together, and when the glue is thoroughly set, smooth down the shape with a surform and finish first with coarse and then fine glasspaper (sandpaper). Put on a coat of emulsion or undercoat and paint it with whatever finish you like. A very small screw eye put into the top makes a ring to hang it by to a ribbon or chain.

The Victorians were also fond of making necklaces from plaques or very small cameos, joined by rings, cords, ribbons or chains. These are quite easy to represent with small shapes cut in ply or even thick card, painted with acrylics and glazed or given a light coloured undercoat and painted over with F.E.V.

38 *War and Peace*, London
Coliseum, 1973. Photo: Donald
Southern. Jewellery made from
stiffened lace, painted and
jewelled

Edwardian

The favourite jewels of the Edwardians were diamonds, closely followed by rubies,
amethysts, sapphires and emeralds. Except for very showy tiaras, necklaces and
bracelets, it really doesn't pay to try to make Edwardian jewellery. For the showy
things, stones and drop-shaped stones look quite effective sewn on to a criss-cross
gold or black net. To make a heavy jewelled necklace cut out the whole shape in flesh-
coloured net and cover it completely with stones, which should be sewn on carefully,
not puckering the net. If the stones are heavy the edge of the net may need wiring to
keep it in shape.

Art Nouveau jewellery was most often enamelled and gold. Leather takes paint
and varnish well and makes a pretty good representation of enamel, if the colours are
well chosen. For a floral design, stalks can be made of wire twisted into shape and
glued or sewn on.

Present day

Plays set in the present do not as a rule contain people who spend a fortune on
jewellery, but if some do have to be coped with it is certainly most satisfactory to hire
some good imitations or buy from Woolworths and adapt. Most older women now
wear 'costume jewellery', which can be bought, or the actresses may be able to provide
their own.

In an absolutely naturalistic play of the present day, there should not be the usual enlargement of scale as it either gives an impression of immense wealth or looks too obviously false. The sort of jewellery worn by young people is probably inexpensive in any case and can usually be bought or borrowed, but it is not at all difficult to mock up out of almost anything to hand. As things are so inventive and extravagant already, it's not too hard to go a little further towards beauty, curiousness or absurdity and to exaggerate a little in size and design.

Wooden or perspex plaques painted with enamel, F.E.V., gold or silver, look splendid. Foil papers, stuck behind or between two layers of perspex, shine through to give a very rich effect. The plaques can be drilled and hung on leather thongs or cords. In stationers and hardware stores many items are displayed in packets, usually hung on racks or on the wall, and a look around these will often stimulate your imagination; so will food shops, where various kinds of beans, macaroni, rice and packaging materials may start a train of thought. From the countryside there are chestnuts, sunflower seeds, acorns, acorn cups, and oak apples. The seashore too is rich in possibilities.

I cannot stress too much or too often the value of invention and imagination. These, combined with some skill and the knowledge of a few basic techniques, can produce almost anything you need.

Some U.S. Equivalents

UK	US
Adhesives	
Araldite	a two-part epoxy adhesive
Bostik 1 and 2	a two-part epoxy adhesive
coldwater paste	wheat paste
Copydex	a latex binding adhesive (as sold by Rug Craft hobby stores)
Cow Gum	a rubber cement
Evostick Impact 528	a contact cement (e.g. Weldwood)
Polycell	a vinyl wallpaper paste (e.g. Rex Paste)
Scotch or pearl glue	carpenters' or ground glue
Tretobond 37	a rubber-based panel
Uhu	aeroplane glue
Fireproofing	
Albi-clear (for plastics)	Fire-Tect PC-225
Solution N5	Fire-Tect W1
Materials	
alabastine	spackle
butter muslin	cheese cloth
calico	muslin
cartridge paper	construction paper
casting foam	flexible urethane foam
cellulose filler	Cell-u-clay
cinemoid	Roscolene
deal	pine
Dutch metal	imitation metal leaf
foam plastic	flexible urethane foam
gauze	net
hessian	burlap
holland linen	a good quality heavy linen
lurex	plastic metallic fabric
Neofol	aluminium foil
nylon crin	nylon bobbinet
perspex	plexiglas
ply	plywood
Polyfilla	Gypsum
polystyrene	expanded polystyrene foam (e.g. styrofoam, Dorvon)
polythene	polyurethane
scrim	scenic gauze
skin ply	Easy Curve
stockinet	thin cotton jersey
sugar paper	absorbent construction paper
Supertoe	Celastic
timber	lumber
timber merchants	lumber yard
Vinamould	Plastico-Moulace
Paints, mediums and glazes	
button polish	a sticky, honey-brown polish for which there is no real equivalent in the US. Use lacquer except where indicated otherwise
emulsion paint/glaze	vinyl/acrylic paint/glaze
Evostick Resin w	a solvent base PVA
scenic powder colour	dry scenic color
Tenaxatex	a solvent base PVA
Unibond	white glue (e.g. Elmers Glue-All)
Vandyke crystals	analine dye
white polish	shellac
Miscellaneous	
backcloth	backdrop
blow torch	propane torch
formers	supports
fretsaw	scroll saw
gimp pins	brads or wire nails
glasspaper	sandpaper
hire	rent
hire firm	rental house
methylated spirits	industrial or wood alcohol
mouth spray	atomizer
pegs	pins
Scara-web	plastic netting
Sellotape	plastic or colored cloth adhesive tape
Stanley knife	matt knife

Book List

Bergstrom, Ingvar *Dutch Still Life Painting in the Seventeenth Century* Faber and Faber, London 1956

Bossert, Helmuth *Folk Art in Europe* A. Zwemmer Ltd, London 1954

Bott, Alan *Our Fathers* William Heinemann, London 1932

Bott, Alan *Our Mothers* Victor Gollancz, London 1932

Boucher, Francois *History of Costume in the West* Thames and Hudson, London 1967

Caldecott, Randolph *Graphic Pictures* George Routledge, London 1883

Davenport, Millia *The Book of Costume* Crown Publishers, New York 1948

Digby, George Wingfield *The Devonshire Hunting Tapestries* (in the Victoria and Albert Museum) Her Majesty's Stationery Office, London 1971

Evans, Joan (ed.) *The Flowering of the Middle Ages* Thames and Hudson, London 1966

Fischel, Dr Oskar and von Boehn, Max *Modes and Manners* J. M. Dent, London 1927

Le Grammaire des Styles Librairie Ernest Flammarion, Paris
Many volumes on artistic styles of various countries.

Hartley, Dorothy and Elliot, Margaret M. *The Life and Work of the People of England.* 2 vols. B. T. Batsford Ltd, London 1925

Janneau, Gillaume *Les Arts Decoratifs*: a) *Le Luminaire* b) *Les Sieges* c) *Les Meubles* 3 vols. Librairie Ernest Flammarion, Paris

Lipman, Jean *American Folk Decoration* Dover Publications Inc., New York 1951

Maurois, André *An Illustrated History of England* The Bodley Head, London 1963

Mediaeval England 2 vols. Clarendon Press, Oxford 1917

Morse, H. K. *Elizabethan Pageantry 1560–1620* Studio Ltd, London 1934

Praz, Mario *Conversational Pieces* Methuen, London 1971

Praz, Mario *An Illustrated History of Interior Decoration* Thames and Hudson, London 1964

The Reader's Digest Complete Do It Yourself Manual Reader's Digest Association, London 1969

Scott-Giles, C. W. *Shakespeare's Heraldry* J. M. Dent, London 1950

Shakespeare's England 2 vols. Clarendon Press, Oxford 1916

Sources of Supplies

UK

The places listed below are those which have proved most useful to the contributors to this book, but as so many businesses are moving away from the centre in search of cheaper premises, it is best to check by telephone before making a trip, and it is also sensible to check that they still stock what you need.

There is a publication called Contacts, *brought out quarterly by Spotlight, 42–43 Cranbourne Street, WC2, Tel. 01-437 7631, which contains an enormous amount of information on where to buy and hire properties and furniture and where to get props or structures made professionally.*

Acetate
J. DENNY AND CO. (large sheets of perspex, resin, blocks, tube, etc) 13 Netherwood Road W14 01-603 5152
DUNN AND CO. 44 Newman Street W1 01-636 8811
COBEX (Fireproof) G. H. Bloore 68 Willow Walk Bermondsey SE1 01-237 8271

Antique and Secondhand Shops
Groups of these can be found in the following areas:
Camden High Street NW1
Camden Passage Islington High Street and Upper Street N1
Church Street and Church Walk Kensington
Kings Road and Fulham Road Chelsea (the Putney end)
Portobello Road Westbourne Grove W11 and other roads in that area

Artificial Flowers and Plants
FLORAL DECOR (artificial flowers made to order) 53 Brewer Street W1 01-437 1957

GREEN FINGERS (also supply real flowers)   264 Brixton Hill SW2   01-674 9425
The big department stores also sell good plastic flowers

Baskets
GREENWICH WORKSHOPS   166 Greenwich High Road SE10   01-858 0316
MERCHANT CHANDLER   72 New King's Road SW6   01-736 6141
UNITED WORKSHOP FOR THE BLIND   47 Victoria Street SW1   01-222 5741

Buttons and Trimmings, etc
ELLS AND FARRIER (beads, buttons, trimmings, sequins, braids)   5 Princes Street W1   01-629 9964
M. HAND & CO. LTD (military braids, etc)   25 Lexington Street W1   01-437 4917
PARKER (TOGGLES) LTD (rivets, brass buckles, etc)   39 Wilson Street Finsbury Square EC2 01-606 8629

Card and Paper, etc
SAMUEL JONES LTD (self-adhesive)   40/50 Mansell Street E1   01-709 0791
F. G. KETTLE BROS. (all sorts of coloured and metallic paper, acetate, heavy card and boxes)   127 High
    Holborn WC1   01-405 9764
PAPERCHASE (all sorts)   216 Tottenham Court Road W1   01-637 1121

Electrical and Lighting, Lamps, Chandeliers, etc
J.M.B. HIRE COMPANY   52a Goldhawk Road W12   01-743 7867
CHRISTOPHER WRAY LIGHTING EMPORIUM (excellent period lamps)   600 King's Road SW6   01-736 8008

Fabric Dyes and Paints
BRODIE AND MIDDLETON   79 Long Acre WC2   01-836 3289
THE COSMIC CRAYON COMPANY Bedford (fabric crayons)   Obtainable from Reeves, Hamleys, Selfridges
DE VILBISS COMPANY LTD (spray guns, etc)   Ringwood Road Bournemouth BH11 9L   020-16 3131
DYLON INTERNATIONAL LTD   Lower Sydenham Road SE26 5HD   01-650 4801
I.C.I. DYESTUFFS DIVISION   Hexagon House Blackley Manchester
GEORGE ROWNEY AND CO. LTD   12 Percy Street W1   01-636 8241
SELASTASINE SILK SCREENS LTD   22 Bulstrode Street W1   01-935 0768
SERICOL GROUP LTD (screen printing inks)   24 Parsons Green SW6   01-736 8181
WINSOR AND NEWTON LTD   52 Rathbone Place W1   01-636 4231

Feathers
MISS RHULE   9 Lower John Street W1   01-485 1620
MR W. F. SOWERBY   7 Newbury Street EC1   01-606 2114

Felt
B. BROWN (HOLBORN) LTD FELTS   32 Greville Street EC1   01-242 4311
BURY FELT COMPANY   23/24 Old Bailey   01-248 3606
FLETCHER NEWMAN LTD   Shelton House Shelton Street WC2   01-240 1726

Fibre Glass and Resin
BRODIE AND MIDDLETON   See **Fabric Dyes and Paints**
STRAND GLASS (also supplies Aerosol Powder)   109 High Street Brentford Middlesex   01-568 7191
ALEC TIRANTI   21 Goodge Place W1   01-636 8565

Fire Proofing
ALBI-CLEAR L.B. LABORATORIES LTD (to paint on)   Felcourt East Grinstead Surrey   0342 23661
ALUMATE INDUSTRIES LTD (for Agricol)   22 Henrietta Street WC2   01-236 0451
FLAMEBAR (spray)   Bernard Collins Hillview Works Manor Way Boreham Wood Herts   01-953 1752
SELLESTA FLAME PROOFING LTD   222 Archway Road N6   01-340 3043

Foil
BORDEN CHEMICAL COMPANY (U.K.) LTD   Marsh Lane Ware Herts   0920 2394/2395

Furniture Rentals and Sales
G. AUSTIN AND SONS LTD (sales only)   29 Peckham Rye SE15   01-639 3163 and 39 Brayards Road SE15
    01-639 0480
LOUIS KOCH AND SONS (hire)   106 Cleveland Street W1   01-387 8426
OLD TIMES FURNISHING (hire)   135 Lower Richmond Road SW15   01-788 3551
S. AND T.V. (hire)   Farm Street Fulham SW6   01-381 3511
SUPERHIRE (hire)   2/10 Telford Way Acton W3 7XS   01-749 3787
W. AND M. PRODUCTION FURNISHING LTD (hire)   Unit 5 (2) Industrial Estate Hythe Road NW10
    01-969 6615

Glass Eyes
DALE GLASS EYE COMPANY LTD   Angel House Pentonville Road N1   01-837 1994

Glues
NATIONAL ADHESIVES LTD   Slough Bucks   75-29191
SPRAY GLUE   Piccadilly Photo Centre 16 Piccadilly Arcade SW1   01-499 4617

Hardware and Tools
ROBERT DYAS LTD   5 Botolph Street EC3   01-283 8435
ALEX HAWKINS AND SONS LTD   125 London Road SE1   01-928 6682

Jewellery Hire
ROBINSONS   76 Neal Street WC2   01-240 01100

Leather, Leather Dyes and Tools, etc
ABBEY LEATHERS   1 Crescent Row (off Baltic Street) EC1   01-253 4701
B. AND G. LEATHER CLOTH   17 Fairfax Road NW6 4EE   01-624 8100

CHAMOIS LEATHER COMPANY   169 Bermondsey Street E1   01-407 1266
F. W. COLLINS (belts, thick leather, tools, etc)   14 Earlham Street WC2   01-836 3964
LIGHT LEATHER COMPANY LTD   16 Soho Square W1   01-437 5782/3

Markets
ANTIQUARIUS MARKET   King's Road Chelsea
ANTIQUE HYPERMARKET   Kensington High Street
ANTIQUE SUPERMARKET   St Christopher's Place W1
BERMONDSEY   Tower Bridge Road   Fridays 7am–2.30pm
CAMDEN PASSAGE N1   Saturdays
THE CHELSEA MARKET   King's Road Chelsea
CHURCH STREET NW8   Saturdays
PETTICOAT LANE and BRICK LANE near Aldgate and Whitechapel   Sunday mornings
THE PORTOBELLO ROAD W11   Saturdays; cheaper at the end furthest from Notting Hill Gate

Metal
AERO NAUTICAL MODELS (fine rods and wires etc, for model making)   Parkway NW1   01-485 1818
BEDFORD STEER END AND CO. LTD (metal weavers, mesh, etc)   74 Long Lane SE1   01-407 2268
BONDS LTD (rods and wires)   Rumbold Hill Midhurst Sussex   07-3081 3441
ENTERPRISE METAL CO.   84 Great Suffolk Street SE1   01-928 1963
P. E. KEMP   Canbury Park Road Kingston-upon-Thames Surrey   01-549 1124
THORP MODEL MAKERS (rods and wires)   98 Gray's Inn Road WC1   01-405 1016

Novelty Goods
BARNETT NOVELTY   17 Kensington Park Road W11   01-727 7164
BARNUMS   67 Hammersmith Road W14   01-602 1211
F. BECK   22 Camden Passage N1   01-226 3403

Ornamental Hardware
WILLIAM BEARDMORE AND CO. LTD (architectural ironmongers)   4 Percy Street W1   01-636 1214
COMYN CHING AND CO. LTD   15 Shelton Street WC2   01-836 9123
FRANK ROMNEY   52 Camden High Street NW1   01-387 2579

Padding
WOOLFIN AND SONS LTD (Dacron)   11 Old Street EC1   01-253 3140

Plaster, Clay and Sculptors' Supplies
BRITISH GYPSUM LTD   15 Marylebone Road NW1   01-486 1282
L. CORNELISSON AND SONS   22 Great Queen Street WC2   01-405 3304
ALEC TIRANTI   See **Fibre Glass and Resin**

Plastics
COTTRELL AND CO., Dental Material Manufacturers   15 Charlotte Street W1   01-580 5500
ELASTOMER PRODUCTS (for expanding foam plastic)   Warf Way Glen Parva Leicester LE2 9TF   053-726 769
G.W. FILM SALES (styrene/bextrene sheets, etc)   Brittania Works 8 Keller Road Woolwich Industrial Estate SE28 0AX   01-855 9531
PASSMORE STYROFORM (polystyrene)   12 Merrow Street E14   01-790 6501
SWAINS PACKAGING (polythene)   Buckhurst Hill Essex   01-504 9151

Rubber
BELLAMAN, IVEY AND CARTER (latex)   358 Grand Drive SW20   01-540 1372
PENTONVILLE RUBBER COMPANY LTD   52 Pentonville Road N1   01-837 4582

Scenic Canvas, Gauze, Hessian, etc
J. D. MCDOUGALL (also supplies mesh in many sizes)   64 Station Road Forest Gate E7   01-534 2921
RUSSELL AND CHAPPELL LTD (also webbing)   23 Monmouth Street WC2   01-836 7521

Scenic Paints and Dry Pigments
BRODIE AND MIDDLETON LTD (also F.E.V.)   See **Fabric Dyes**
HILL-JONES THOMAS LTD   15 High Street E15   01-534 2761
JOHN T. KEMP   15 Theobalds Road WC1   01-242 7578
A. LEETE AND CO. LTD   129 London Road SE1   01-928 5283

Sheet Metal
J. SMITH AND SONS (Clerkenwell Ltd) (non-ferrous)   50 St John's Square EC1   01-253 1277

Studio Supplies
CHELSEA ART STORES   314 King's Road SW3   01-352 0430
LETRASET   44 Gerrard Street W1   01-437 3242
REEVES AND SONS LTD   13 Charing Cross Road WC2   01-930 9940
C. ROBERSON AND CO. LTD   77 Parkway NW1   01-485 0025 and 01-267 2068
GEORGE ROWNEY AND CO. LTD   See **Fabric Dyes**
WINSOR AND NEWTON LTD   See **Fabric Dyes**

Technical Drawing Equipment (See also **Studio Supplies**)
THE DRAWING OFFICE CENTRE (Amdel)   Abbey House Victoria Street SW1   01-222 5656
DRAWING OFFICE MATERIALS MANUFACTURERS AND DEALERS ASSOCIATION   171 Victoria Street SW1   01-834 9382
THORP MODEL MAKERS   See **Metal**
UNIVERSAL DRAWING OFFICE LTD   5 Bloomsbury Square WC1   01-242 8776
The last three organisations also make die-line prints

Weapons and Armour
REG AMOS   The National Theatre   01-928 2033

BAPTY AND CO. LTD (hire only)   9 Macklin Street WC2 9HX   01-405 2021
ROBERT WHITE AND SONS   25 Shelton Street WC2   01-835 8237

Wood Suppliers
J. J. AND S. W. CHALK   32 Commercial Road E1   01-709 1706
LATCHFORD TIMBER MERCHANTS   61 Endell Street WC2   01-836 6556

US

The following addresses have been compiled as a helpful indication of where many major suppliers can be found. In cases where mail order houses are involved, zip codes have been supplied. For more complete listings readers should consult Simon's Directory, *published by Package Publicity Service, 1564 Broadway, New York, N.Y. 10036;* Theatre Crafts Magazine, *published by Rodale Press, Emmaus, P.A. 18049; and the local yellow pages.*

Adhesives
GULF SPECIALTIES   1430 W Victorson   Houston, Texas
THE 3 M COMPANY   3 M Center   St Paul, Minnesota   or
   15 Henderson Drive   West Caldwell, New Jersey
PLASTICS SUPPLY COMPANY   2401 E 40th Avenue   Denver, Colorado
MANHATTAN ADHESIVES CORPORATION   425 Greenspoint Avenue   Brooklyn, New York
SLOMONS LABS INC.   32–45 Hunters Point Avenue   Long Island City, New York
YATES PRODUCTS   711 Ivy Street   Glendale, California

Art Supplies
ART WORLD   230 Central Park Westroads   Omaha, Nebraska
ERIKSEN'S CRAFTS INC.   50 Highway and 83 Street   Kansas City, Missouri
GOLDEN ARTISTS MATERIALS   2525 Broadway   New York
M. GRUMBACHER INC.   460 West 34th Street   New York
PEARL PAINT CO. INC.   308 Canal Street   New York
SHELDON'S   200 East Ohio   Chicago, Illinois

Artificial Flowers and Plants
CALLAHAMS   2130 Welton   Denver, Colorado
CHICAGO FLORIST SUPPLY CO.   1354 West Lake   Chicago, Illinois
ELK SUPPLY CO.   39 West 29th Street   New York
FLOWER CITY   400 2nd Avenue Worth   Minneapolis, Minnesota
FLOWER CITY OF OMAHA   124 Westminister Mall   Westroads   Omaha, Nebraska
INTERNATIONAL MERCHANDIZING CORPORATION   1341 Heights Blvd   Houston, Texas

Baskets
GREENSPAN R. & COMPANY INC.   39 Ainslie Street   Brooklyn, New York
HOFFMAN HEIGHTS HARDWARE   660 Peoria   Denver, Colorado
MACRON MARKETING CONCEPTS INC.   200 West 9th Avenue   Kansas City, Missouri
OSTRIN LLOYD   2825 Washington Ave N   Minneapolis, Minnesota
STATE SUPPLY CO. INC.   68 Thomas Street   New York
TRADER HORN   1133 N State   Chicago, Illinois

Blueprinters
A-BLUE PRINT CO.   1657 Westheimer   Houston, Texas
CIRCLE BLUEPRINTERS   225 West 57th Street   New York
INDEPENDENT PRINTERS   215 East 42nd Street   New York
MERIT STUDIOS INC.   250 West 54th Street   New York
NORTH WEST REPRODUCTIONS CO.   7631 Lyndale Avenue South   Minneapolis, Minnesota
PACIFIC BLUE PRINT CO. INC.   3423 West 6th Street   Los Angeles, California

Feathers
A.A. FEATHER CO.   38 West 38th Street   New York
AMERICAN TRIMMING HOUSE   223 West Mulberry   Baltimore, Maryland
ARIZONA COSTUME HOUSE   4240 N 19th Avenue   Phoenix, Arizona
CHARLES ZUCKER CORPORATION   31 Mercer Street   New York
RAINBOW FEATHER DYEING CO.   3210 N San Fernando Blvd.   Burbank, California
SCHWARTZ M. & SON   321 East 3rd Street   New York

Felt
BEN FRANKLIN STORE ENGLEWOOD   10923 Winner Road   Kansas City, Missouri
CENTRAL SHIPPEE   24 West 25th Street   New York
FELT & CHENILLE MFG CO.   20 N High   Akron, Ohio
FOSS M.L. INC.   1901 Arap   Denver, Colorado
G.A.F. FELT PRODUCTS   G.A.F. Corporation   11653 Adie Road   St Louis, Missouri
SUPERIOR FELT CORPORATION   1910 Highland   Kansas City, Missouri

Fibre Glass
ALLIED FIBERGLASS CO.   2120 Colfax Avenue   Denver, Colorado
BERTON PLASTICS   170 Wesley   South Hackensack, New Jersey
COASTAL FIBERGLASS CO.   914 South Shaver   Houston, Texas
FIBERCHEM INC.   3549 NW Yeon   Portland, Oregon
INDUSTRIAL ARTS SUPPLY (mail order)   5724 W 36th Street   Minneapolis, Minnesota
INDUSTRIAL PLASTICS   324 Canal Street   New York

Fireproofing
FIRE-TECT INC.   3235 Whiteside Street   L.A., California 90063

Foam Rubber

A-1 FOAM RUBBER SPECIALTY CO.   7608 Lyndale Ave South   Minneapolis, Minnesota
BERNARD DOBNER FOAM RUBBER   1987 Jerome Avenue   Bronx, New York
CLARK RUBBER PRODUCTS   3838 Grant Street   Omaha, Nebraska
FOAM CRAFTS PRODUCTION CO.   1164 Old Main   Akron, Ohio
FOAM RUBBER CO.   807 H Street NW   Washington D.C.
PARAMOUNT FOAM & SPONGE MATERIALS   1711 South Second   Piscataway, New Jersey

Foil

DEMAC CORPORATION   45 Bloomingdale Road   Hicksville, New York
ECKO PRODUCTS INC.   17–38 State Highway No. 208   Fair Lawn, New Jersey
KAISER ALUMINUM & CHEMICAL SALES   3033 Executive Blvd   Minneapolis, Minnesota
ST REGIS PAPER COMPANY   Laminated & Coated Prod. Div.   100 S Wacker Drive   Chicago, Illinois
    or   235 East 31 Street   New York

Glass Eyes (See also Novelty Goods)

ALLIN'S TAXIDERMY STUDIO   127 East Lexington   Kansas City, Missouri
CHAUVIN'S STUDIO   4417 White Plain Road   Bronx, New York
HOFFMAN M.J. COMPANY   963 Broadway   Brooklyn, N.Y.
REEL TROPHY   6435 SW Burlingame Place   Portland, Oregon

Latex Rubber

EXXON CHEMICAL COMPANY U.S.A.   1333 West Loop South   Houston, Texas
FOAM CRAFTS PRODUCTION CO.   See Foam Rubber
REICHHOLD CHEMICAL INC.   2508 Bailey   Akron, Ohio
RUBBER LATEX CO. OF AMERICA   210 Delawavna Avenue   Clifton, New Jersey
TORCH RUBBER CO. INC.   3775 10th Avenue   New York

Leather Supplies

BERMAN LEATHER COMPANY (full line of leather, over 350 styles of buckles, tools, dyes)   147 South
    Street   Boston, Mass. 02111
LEATHER & SUPPLY   1409 South Los Angeles Street   Los Angeles, California
LEATHERCRAFTERS SUPPLY CO. (mail order—full line of leather, tools, dyes)   25 Great Jones Street
    New York, N.Y. 10012
TANDY LEATHERS (free mail order catalog—over 200 stores in U.S.)   P.O. Box 2686   Fort Worth,
    Texas 76101

Lighting Equipment   See Multiple Supply Houses

Metal Screens

CAMBRIDGE WIRE CLOTH CO.   7009 Long Drive   Houston, Texas
GERARD DANIEL & CO. INC.   5 Plain Avenue   New Rochelle, N.Y.
ESTERY WIRE WORKS CO.   134 W Central Blvd   Palisades Park, New Jersey
RON VIK INC.   800 Colorado Avenue S   Minneapolis, Minnesota
SHAKER SCREENS   P.O. Box 1   Fenton, Missouri
TETKO INC.   525 S Monterey Pass Road   Monterey Park, California

Metal Work

B. & E. IRON WORKS   6307 West Grand Avenue   Chicago, Illinois
IRON WORKS INC.   1926 S 2nd Street   Hopkins, Minnesota
THE ORNAMENTAL IRON MFG CO.   3419 North 30th Street   Omaha, Nebraska
NORTH EAST FABRICATORS   1759 West Farm Road   Bronx, New York
SALVO IRON WORKS   2368 Bathgate Avenue   Bronx, New York
TOWER IRON WORKS INC.   2322 Bissonnet   Houston, Texas

Multiple Supply Houses

The following companies carry a full line of products including: fabrics, hardware and tools, lighting
equipment, paints, props, plus many other items. Catalogs are usually available upon request

AMERICAN SCENIC CO.   11 Andrew Street   Greensville, South Carolina
MUTUAL HARDWARE CORPORATION   5–45 49th Avenue   Long Island City, New York
NORCOSTCO INC.   3203 N Highway 100   Minneapolis, Minnesota
OLESEN COMPANY   1535 Ivar Avenue   Hollywood, California
PARAMOUNT THEATRICAL SUPPLIES   32 West 20th Street   New York
STAGE ENGINEERING & SUPPLY INC.   P.O. Box 2002   Colorado Springs, Colorado
TOBIN LAKE STUDIOS   2650 Seven Mile Road   South Lyon, Michigan

Novelty Goods

DENNISON PARTY BAZAAR   390 5th Avenue   New York
GORDON NOVELTY COMPANY   933 Broadway   New York
HOOKER-HOWE COSTUME COMPANY   46–52 S Main Street   Haverhill, Mass.
IMITATION FOOD DISPLAY COMPANY   197 Waverly Avenue   Brooklyn, New York
INVINCIBLE SALES CORPORATION   2303 West 9th Street   Los Angeles, California
MAGIC CENTER   739 8th Avenue   New York

Ornamental Hardware

ACME HARDWARE   150 South La Brea Avenue   Los Angeles, California
DECORATIVE ACCESSORIES INC.   1934 South Taylor   Akron, Ohio
DECORATIVE HARDWARE   Nob Hill in the Galleria   3494 West 70th   Minneapolis, Minnesota
GARGOYLE (antique hardware)   1023 Olive   Shreveport, Louisiana
WILLIAM HUNRATH CO.   153 East 57th Street   New York
SIMON'S HARDWARE INC.   421 Third Avenue   New York

Plastics
AMERICAN CYANAMID CO.   7630 Executive Blvd   Minneapolis, Minnesota
COMMERCIAL PLASTICS AND SUPPLY CORP.   7406 Lawndale   Houston, Texas
GEM-O-LITE PLASTICS   5525 Cahvenga   North Hollywood, California
OMAHA PLASTICS   1470 South 16th   Omaha, Nebraska
PLASTICS FACTORY   119 Avenue D   New York   N.Y. 10009
TENNECO CHEMICALS INC.   Foams and Plastic Division   640 West 134th Street   Bronx, New York

Scenic Canvas   See **Multiple Supply Houses**

Scenic Fabric
ART DRAPERY STUDIOS   2766 N Lincoln Avenue   Chicago, Illinois
ASSOCIATED FABRICS   10 East 39th Street   New York
ASTRUP COMPANY   P.O. Box 535 Raritan Center   12 Parkway Place   Edison, New York
ATLANTA COSTUME COMPANY   2089 Monroe NE   Atlanta, Georgia
DAZIAN'S INC.   40 East 29th Street   New York   or   2014 Commerce Street   Dallas, Texas

Scenic Lumber
DYKES LUMBER   1901 Park Avenue   Weehawken, New Jersey
GANCEDO LUMBER COMPANY   9300 NW 36th Avenue   Miami, Florida
GOTHIC LUMBER AND MILLWORK INC.   698 Second Avenue   New York
KNOX LUMBER COMPANY   6973 West Broadway   Minneapolis, Minnesota
TEXAS SCENIC COMPANY   Box 28297   San Antonio, Texas

Sheet Metal
ABRAMOWITZ TINSMITH SUPPLY CORP.   717 Southern Blvd   Bronx, New York
BLUMENTHAL SHEET METAL   1206 Chapman Street   Houston, Texas
FABRICATING EQUIPMENT AND SYSTEMS INC.   3601 Park Center Blvd.   Minneapolis, Minnesota
KRUSE METALS MANUFACTURING CO.   1330 Channing Street   Los Angeles, California
S. AND J. SHEET METAL SUPPLY INC.   526 E 134 Street   Bronx, New York

Shell Suppliers
DERBY LANE CENTER   10515 Gandy Boulevard   St Petersberg, Florida
FLORIDA SUPPLY HOUSE   P.O. Box 847   Brandenton, Florida
GOOLENI   11 Riverside Drive   Suite 5 VE   New York
SEASHELL TREASURES   P.O. Box 730   Oakhurst, California

Trimming
AMERICAN TRIMMING HOUSE   223 W Mulberry   Baltimore, Maryland
ARIZONA COSTUME HOUSE   4240 N 19th Avenue   Phoenix, Arizona
ASSOCIATED COSTUME RENTAL   99 Empire   Providence, Rhode Island
DAZIAN'S INC.   See **Scenic Fabric**
LEO'S ADVANCE THEATRICAL CO.   124 N Wabash Avenue   Chicago, Illinois
SALT LAKE COSTUME COMPANY   1701 South 11th East   Salt Lake City, Utah

Weapons and Armour
BROADWAY COSTUME HOUSE   15 W Hubbard   Chicago, Illinois
COSTUME ARMOUR   381 Canal Place   Bronx, New York
COSTUME BAZAAR   26 Grove   New Haven, Connecticut
EXHIBIT BUILDERS   Box 226   Deland, Florida
INVINCIBLE SALES CORPORATION   See **Novelty Goods**

Art as a Source of Ideas

Many works of art show people in different situations and circumstances surrounded by the appurtenances of their way of life, which may be religious, domestic, scholastic or professional, in peace or in war. A list follows—by no means comprehensive—of some of the sources which we have found most useful. Many of the works, especially the early ones, are very formalized but nevertheless give a good idea of how things must have looked.

Pre-Medieval
The tomb painting of ancient Egypt. For furniture, utensils, flora and fauna, in fact most of the things with which men have contact in daily life. The hieroglyphics also contain some useful material
Ancient Greek painted vases
Roman still-lifes and frescoes. For furniture and other domestic details. The mosaics, especially some of those at Ostia, show among other things tools and tradesmen's implements

The Middle Ages
Early illuminated manuscripts, especially the Lutterell Psalter. Rich in information about religious and domestic life

Fifteenth Century
The Limbourg brothers, French illuminators, late 14th and early 15th centuries
Jan van Eyck, Flemish painter, died 1441. His painting of Giovanni Arnolfini and his wife is particularly useful
Nicolas Froment, French painter, active 1450–1490. For interior and exterior décor, etc

Sixteenth Century
Hieronymus Bosch, Dutch painter, 1450–1516. Grotesque detail
Vittore Carpaccio, Italian painter, 1460/5–1523/6. Beautifully detailed interiors and exteriors
Albrecht Dürer, German painter and draughtsman, 1471–1528. Remarkably meticulous detail
Lucas Cranach, German painter, 1472–1553. Especially useful for jewellery
Hans Holbein, German painter and draughtsman, 1497/8–1543. Painted a great deal in England
Pieter Bruegel, Flemish painter, 1525/30–1569. Peasants feasting, dancing and working

Seventeenth Century
Caravaggio, Italian painter, 1573–1610
Frans Snyders, Flemish painter, 1579–1627. Still-lifes
The Le Nain brothers, French painters, spanning the years 1588–1677. Peasant and farm life and bourgeois life
Peter Lely, English painter, 1618–1680. Jewellery
The seventeenth century was the great age of the Dutch interior and still-life painters, some of the most interesting of whom are the following:
Abraham Bosse, engraver, 1602–1676
Emanuel de Witte, 1617–1692
Jan Steen, 1626–1679
Pieter de Hooch, 1629–1685
Gabriel Metsu, 1629/30–1667
Esias Boursse, 1631–1672
Jan Vermeer, 1632–1675

Eighteenth Century
Antoine Watteau, French painter, 1684–1721. Musical instruments, etc
William Hogarth, English engraver, 1697–1764. Mostly low life
Antonio Canaletto, Italian painter, 1797–1768. Painted many works in England as well as in Venice
Jean Baptiste Chardin, French painter, 1699–1779. Domestic scenes and still lifes
Pietro Longhi, Italian painter, 1702–1785. Domestic scenes from different social classes
Francesco Guardi, Italian painter, 1712–1793. Venetian exteriors and palace interiors, and shipping
Wright of Derby, English painter, 1734–1797. Painted artificial light
Johann Zoffany, English painter, 1725–1810. Conversation pieces, mostly upper classes

Nineteenth Century
Honoré Daumier, French painter, lithographer and caricaturist, 1808–1879. Low life and the life of the law courts
Gustave Courbet, French painter, 1819–1877
The French Impressionists, especially:
Edgar Degas, 1834–1917
Paul Cézanne, 1839–1906
Auguste Renoir, 1841–1919

Index

Entries in bold refer to half-tone illustration numbers.